THE ENNEAGRAM LETTERS

THE
ENNEAGRAM
LETTERS

A Poetic Exploration of
Who You Thought You Had to Be

SARAJANE CASE

Andrews McMeel
PUBLISHING®

CONTENTS

INTRODUCTION

As life moves forward, we collect titles like categorization lint rollers. Every choice we make adds another clarifier onto our personality: parent, child, spouse, student, employee, type A/type B, introvert/extrovert, what you want to be when you grow up, what you do for a living, and so on.

Grabbing them up, unconsciously and consciously adding to the way we see and express ourselves. Adding to how others see and understand us. At times this feels useful. We're given a sense of understanding—of not being alone. It provides language for how we tell people who we are: "Hi, I'm Sarajane, a stepmom, business owner, and extrovert who prefers to be alone and loves good coffee." This starts to take the place of getting to know one another and ourselves in intricate and complex ways. These categories so easily go from helpful to stifling in a matter of moments, no longer making us feel known and instead doing the opposite—telling us who we are even when we've moved beyond it or no longer experience ourselves that way.

The magic of the Enneagram is not in finding ourselves in these numbers, but rather in recognizing that the things we thought we had to be were never ours to carry.

There is a tremendous amount of relief available to us when we choose to allow ourselves the full range of the human experience, to operate from all nine types and all three centers.

This compilation of poems and essays is here as what I hope to be a soothing balm to the part of you that feels pressured to be perfect, lovable, successful, significant, capable, supported, happy, strong, or easy to get along with in order to have a place on Earth where you belong.

It's like the chrysalis and the butterfly, assuming that there was never anything wrong with the caterpillar. When we live inside of the constraints of our Enneagram type, we are settling for a life in a cocoon. Safe, purposeful, and limited.

This book is a compilation of poems and essays written to the nine different pressures of the Enneagram. The things we think we have to be in life in order to be worthy of love, success, or safety. We explore the idea that we each in our own way, and to varying degrees, experience the gravity of these nine pressures: perfection, like-ability, success, significance, competence, support, happiness, strength, and easygoingness.

Our Enneagram type is the gift we've given ourselves in an attempt to stay safe. It's a beautiful thing that has supported us thus far in life, but at some point, it's time to let it go in order to recognize that what has served us is no longer what we need.

These poems and essays are my love letters, insights, and experiences poured out in response to the suffering I've seen in individuals of different Enneagram types. At times, they're a direct call to action and, at others, a meditative reflection on the type structure. My hope is that they serve as both a challenge and a healing balm in all of our journeys of being human.

The Enneagram Letters are my invitation into your expansion.

WHY I WROTE THIS BOOK

I started my self-help journey when I was really young. My middle school journals are filled with inspirational quotes and clipped-out pages of *Chicken Soup for the Soul* books.

At times, the messages learned through self-help are healing and inspiring. They make us feel more connected to life and to ourselves. Other times, they make us feel like we're failing or like we aren't quite living up to our own standards. With the Enneagram, sometimes it can feel so disorienting that it's hard to tell what's growth and what's obsession.

"Believe in yourself" feels great when you hit a roadblock and need that extra internal motivation to keep pushing. It feels defeating when you are so far away from self-belief that the idea of believing in yourself feels impossible—like a skill you need to learn but have no idea where to start.

"Just keep going" is beautiful when life is hard, and you need to remember to just put one foot in front of the other. But it's debilitating when you are already burned out and what you really need to do is stop going for a second and breathe.

So often, self-help gurus online teach these things like they are magic pills you take to make life better, easier, and more fulfilling—a get-rich-quick scheme for your soul. Yet, they neglect to share the struggles along the way, the ache in your gut when things aren't so easy, and the emotional mountains you climb on this journey.

I see this happen with the Enneagram all the time—even in my own life. We become so focused on the system and finding where we fit into the system and who we are supposed to be that we ignore how it's making us feel. Or simply, we overthink it.

We ask questions, such as, "If I'm unhappy, can I really be a type seven?" Or, "If I'm no longer fearful of conflict, am I truly a type nine?"

This can lead to seeking to overidentify with our type structure to the point that growth isn't possible.

Or . . .

If you're like me, you start to associate your personality with being wrong. Like anything about your type is somehow a problem even though there are some truly beautiful traits you carry related to your Enneagram type. Like enjoying busy-ness feels like a failure when maybe it's just neutral.

In my opinion, self-help is best used from a healthy distance. When we start to examine ourselves under a microscope, things get blurry and weird and a little too intense.

We tend to forget the simple principle that self-help is meant to help us, to make life more enjoyable, and to aid in healthier relationships and better communication. It's not here to make us dizzy with self-awareness and obsessed with perfecting the way we show up in the world.

You are not a project to be tinkered with. You are a living, breathing being who is worthy of a life well lived, and sometimes that means engaging with self-help and, yes, even the Enneagram through the filters of:

"Is this pouring love in?"

"Do I feel expanded by this?"

"Is this a healing balm?"

"Does this nurture me?"

"Is this improving my life?"

And finally, "How can I engage with this in a way that truly supports me?"

Which brings me to the question I want to leave you with as you open the pages of this book: what if there is absolutely nothing wrong with you, and your growth work is simply about letting yourself be the truest, purest, most open version of who you are? How would your relationship to self-help change?

A BRIEF INTRODUCTION TO THE ENNEAGRAM

The Enneagram is a system of nine unique personality types. Each type has a basic fear and motivation that propels them toward common behaviors or interests. These types are the story of who you thought you had to be in order to survive. These types, when we're living in them fully, are a limitation of our potential. They tell us that in order to be loved, we must do certain things or be certain things, ultimately limiting our access to choices that may be better for our overall well-being.

With that in mind, the goal when working with the Enneagram is to release the belief that you must be this one thing and allow for space to be a full expression of who you are. Live not as your Enneagram type, but work toward expanding your definition of self as you come to terms with who you thought you had to be.

THE NINE ENNEAGRAM TYPES

Type One—The Perfectionist

Basic Desire: "I want to be a good person, to have balance, to live in my integrity."

Basic Fear: "I'm afraid of being a bad person, of being evil or corrupt."

Superego Message: "Most of my life, I've believed that I'll be OK if I just do the right thing."

Type Two—The Helper

Basic Desire: "It's important to me that I'm liked."

Basic Fear: "What if no one ever loves me as I am?"

Superego Message: "I often believe that I am as worthy as I am lovable, that my worth is related to how wanted I am."

Type Three—The Achiever

Basic Desire: "It's important to me that I am accepted and viewed as worthwhile."

Basic Fear: "What if I'm only as worthy as what I can achieve?"

Superego Message: "I believe I will be OK as long as I am constantly achieving new things."

Type Four—The Romantic

Basic Desire: "It's important to me that I find an identity that expresses the truth of who I am and helps me find my significance."

Basic Fear: "What if I am not significant in any way?"

Superego Message: "It's the most important thing for me to always be true to who I am."

Type Five—The Observer

Basic Desire: "It's important to me that I am capable, competent, and informed."

Basic Fear: "I most fear being helpless, useless, or overwhelmed."

Superego Message: "I know that I will be OK as long as I have something that I've truly mastered."

Type Six—The Loyal Skeptic

Basic Desire: "It's important to me that I feel secure and supported."

Basic Fear: "I am fearful of being left out on my own; that I will be without support and guidance and won't be able to survive without it."

Superego Message: "I know that I will be OK as long as I know what is expected of me and make a point to follow through with those expectations."

Type Seven—The Enthusiast

Basic Desire: "It's important to me that I remain happy, satisfied, and fulfilled."

Basic Fear: "I am most afraid of being deprived and trapped in negative emotions."

Superego Message: "I know that I will be OK as long as I get my needs met."

Type Eight—The Challenger

Basic Desire: "It's important to me that I am able to determine my own path in life."

Basic Fear: "I am most afraid of being harmed or controlled by others."

Superego Message: "I know that I will be OK as long as I remain strong and powerful."

Type Nine—The Peacemaker

Basic Desire: "It's important to me that I maintain my peace of mind."

Basic Fear: "I worry about creating rifts with people in my life that cannot be repaired."

Superego Message: "I know that I will be OK as long as those around me are OK."

If you want to read more about the Enneagram and how to work with it for personal growth, I encourage you to pick up a copy of my book *The Honest Enneagram.*

CHAPTER ONE

*

*To the part of you that feels
it must be perfect.*

INTRODUCTION TO TYPE ONE

The Enneagram type one is commonly referred to as "the perfectionist" or "the reformer." They are disciplined, moderate, detail-oriented, and scrupulous. This chapter is dedicated to the part in all of us that never quite feels like we've done enough, the part that questions when the work is done and seeks to live above reproach. In this chapter, we will address complex elements related to the Enneagram type one structure, such as:

1. **The pressure to maintain a high level of performance in day-to-day tasks**
At times, type ones may feel as though they have figured out the best way to do most things, from how to do the grocery shopping to how to drive the car. They put so much focus and attention on refining and perfecting the things they do that it can be overwhelming for themselves and for others. It's great to know the best way to do things. Most of the "best ways," however, end up being much more work than necessary. The type one may end up in a kind of self-created maze of overcomplicated tasks. This leaves them little time for rest and creates an undercurrent of irritation when the people in their life don't do things the way that the type one would.

2. **The harsh inner critic**
Many type ones express having an inner voice that tells them when they've fallen short. The voice may sound like a harsh inner critic, but it can also

sound like the voice of reason or even the voice of God. One might call it an internal system of checks and balances that serves to keep type ones in line. The trouble with this is that, often, the voice isn't very kind—it reminds the type one that they are never enough, that they are always at risk of falling short. It can also be a major source of exhaustion for many type ones. It tells the story that they're never quite done working and should never get too comfortable.

3. The moderating and restricting of access to pleasure and rest

With a heavy focus on being good and doing the right thing, type ones may have almost a resistance to pleasure. They pride themselves on being moderate and sensible, which can make things that feel good seem frivolous or childlike. Many type ones feel like they had to grow up too soon— becoming an adult at a very young age. This sensation can continue into adulthood with the internal messaging that they are the only adult in the room, the pressure to always be the sensible one. Because of this, pleasure for pleasure's sake feels wrong or bad. Like they should be ashamed of feeling that good.

4. The fear of being a bad person and the shame in being "caught" in imperfection

When we hear the term "perfectionist" we can easily believe that means type ones are focused on keeping a clean home, performing perfectly on projects, and keeping track of every grammar mistake. This can be how some type ones experience the type structure; however, the deeper experience is in their striving for moral perfection. They seek to know the right way to do things and continually make choices that keep them above reproach. They are often so hypervigilant in making sure they are doing the right thing that being told they could improve or asked to do it a different way can feel like being caught doing something wrong. Like they should be ashamed of themselves. This is difficult because it makes relationships hard to manage when the type one needs to be right. It also makes it hard for them to find peace if they can never be caught off guard.

5. The perfecting of others

I like the title "reformer" for type one, because I think it very accurately describes the focus of attention we find in this type structure. It's almost like a scanning for what could be improved and an impulse to fix it. This is great in theory, but it's a struggle when it comes to relationships. This type structure focuses on what could be improved in those surrounding a type one, and they often make a point to share that with the people in their life. From what I've learned with talking to type ones, it's not a need to critique as much as it is that the type one thinks you'd want to be in the know—such as, you have spinach in your teeth and it's a type one's duty to make sure you don't go out in public like that. They would want to know if they were doing something their inner critic said was embarrassing, so you must want to know too.

6. The black-and-white thinking

The type one structure often sees the world through a black-and-white lens. Things are either right or wrong, good or bad, and there is very little room for the messy in-between. They may struggle to see differing perspectives and admit when they are wrong. There is so much pressure on them to be morally correct that they create a clear-cut design of what the right thing is to never be caught off guard. They seek this kind of clarity from others as well. A type one in the workplace is going to want clear expectations and obvious delegation so they can ensure that they're doing the right thing.

Although they were written with the type one structure in mind, these essays and poems are an invitation to explore the part in each of us that feels the need to uphold a very high standard of good and right and enough. My hope is that they give you more permission to rest, greater access to self-forgiveness, and an invitation to experience more pleasure in your day-to-day life.

breathe in "I love you."

I have a practice I do when my shoulders grow tight up to my ears, when anger feels hot in my chest or embarrassment burns like lava in my cheeks. It came one night as I was trying to fall asleep, and my mind was chasing the day that was to come like it could tackle the itinerary on its own. I simply breathed in and thought, "I love you," then I breathed out and thought, "It's OK that you're worried." And it felt so comforting I tried it again, breathing in, "I love you," and out, "Tomorrow will be OK." It helped me so much in my process of falling asleep that I began to bring it into other parts of my day—

Sitting on the front porch worried about how well I will handle the things expected of me:

breathe in

"I love you."

and out

"You are equipped to handle all that comes your way."

breathe in

"I love you."

and out

"You are safe to feel the fullness of your fear."

In line at the grocery store frustrated by the lack of speed and then ashamed for not honoring the difficulty of understaffed workplaces during this time:

breathe in

"I love you."

and out

"You can feel empathy and discomfort at the same time."

In a difficult conversation with my partner about a dinner I didn't feel up to:

breathe in

"I love you."

and out

"You are safe."

breathe in

"I love you."

and out

"You love him."

The end of a conversation when my ears are ringing with something I wish I'd left unsaid:

breathe in

"I love you."

and out

"No one else is thinking that much about it."

breathe in

"I love you."

and out

"You asked really good questions."

My breath is the carrier pigeon of loving words flowing in and out of my heart—breathing in love and breathing out comfort. It's so different than the voice I was trained to have in childhood.

This voice—the voice of my breath—I imagine to be a comforting mother-like figure whose thumb gently grazes my forehead as I fall asleep, reminding me I am safe to feel and she would watch over me while I regained energy to do another day.

The voice of my childhood was more like a stiffened school marm; one who carried a ruler around to slap my wrist if she saw me slouch in my seat, a frigid witch of a woman who didn't think I was worthy of joy much at all. If she has to be miserable, then I should be miserable too.

It wouldn't matter how hard I worked or how much I accomplished, my school marm inner voice would notice the single missed punctuation in an otherwise perfect poem.

My breath when she was in charge felt more like a holding. Anger and irritation writhed in my chest while I tried to keep it all together for everything that needed to be done.

For her, I was never enough, and she wouldn't let a moment pass without reminding me of that.

I talk of her like she is a thing of the past, like her influence no longer fazes me, but the truth is the soothing voice of my inner mother is just a bit louder right now. The marm is still writhing in the corner wanting her words to take hold out of fear that I will falter or I will fail.

After all, we all three have the same goal—we seek happiness and peace and a sense that all is well with the world—we just choose different paths to get there. The marm, just like the mother, seeks nothing but good for me, and that's what made her so easy to believe. She must be right that I am not good enough, because she has my best interest at heart. Now, though, I've learned to see her fear for what it really is—disbelief that we can be broken yet still worthy of good things, or even that we were never truly broken at all. That ridges and cracks and missed punctuation are just part of being whole.

That's the wisdom that the mother holds: the truth that we are worthy, that our fullness isn't to be feared, and that the only way to do anything great is to make a lot of mistakes.

So when the school marm screams my misgivings in my ear:

breathe in

"I love you."

and out

"Have no fear."

If your honest emotional expression were a river.

I see your feet planted firmly on the ground
Shoulder pressed hard against a dam
Using all your might to keep the water from tumbling out.

Each tiny leak reminding you to push harder.
Get more strict.
More controlled.

But, a river was never meant to be contained
And nature always takes what is hers.
And your feelings were never meant to be disciplined.

So, the dam comes crashing down—your defenses powerless to
    the pressure
And under the water you go.
First scrambling and fighting as the current takes you in.

But eventually
If you are able to stop resisting and let the river run its course
You will find that it's much easier to float
Than to press hard against the inevitable.

Pressure.

My therapist yelled at me once for how often I clean out the fridge.

Well, she questioned me, and it hit so piercingly close to home that it felt like a scream. For weeks, I'd been in her office complaining of how tired I was, how impatient I felt with my partner, and how there never seemed to be enough time.

In passing, I mentioned that I had a Monday routine where I clean out my fridge, plan meals for the week, go to the store, and prep all the fruits and veggies. This was in addition to my regular high-stress work, going to see her, and all the other bits and bobs that go along with being a wife, a business owner, and a mother.

She paused me and said, "You clean out the fridge every single week?"

"Of course." I had never even questioned that before.

"Do you know how often I clean out the fridge? Every few months."

In that moment, I thought of my Saturday routine where I wake up early and make a list of every single thing I can think of that needs to be done and then spend my weekend doing it. All to head into Monday morning, as I'd set it up, and into the rest of the week where I'd inevitably overscheduled myself once again—putting a tick in my mind to figure out how to stop doing that, and by Friday, we'd start all over with the list and the tasks and the doing. It was like I saw my life flash before my eyes, and it was me climbing the ladder to a high dive,

rung

by

rung,

every single week only to jump off and do it all over again.

Being told that I could be a perfectly suitable human being and have food go bad in my fridge felt like quitting a terrible job without giving notice, dramatically untying my apron, tossing it on the counter while throwing my middle finger in the air, and walking out the door in a blaze of glory.

Liberating—but wrong.

It wasn't that I was obsessed with cleaning out my fridge as much as I had taken the time to figure out the best way to meal-plan. If we clean out our fridge before we meal-plan and go to the store, then we know what ingredients we have to make our meals, and we know what we are about to run out of. It was a perfect system. Then we have to prep the veggies and the fruits right away so that they're easy to grab and we don't accidentally let them go bad because we didn't want to prep them in the moment. When cleaning out the fridge the veggie scraps are used to make broth later in the month—nothing goes to waste.

This would be fine if it was the only thing I'd "perfected." But I was making life a sequence of overcomplicated stressors, justified by the fact that they were so well thought out. Everything had a purpose, and it was all done the "right" way.

When I met my husband, he had a habit of stopping at the store every single day. He'd just run to the store, buy the ingredients for whatever meal he planned to make that night, and then he'd go home and make it.

This drove me bananas. I felt like he was wasting time and probably money. So, I came up with my perfect system, and I took the weight of it onto my shoulders, because it was my idea and, quite frankly, because I don't trust anyone else to do it the way that I would do it.

So you may be just as surprised as we were when, in our seventh year of being together, the following words came out of my mouth, "For the next few months, can we go back to doing grocery shopping the way you used to do it when we met?"

For, in this small habit change, I was able to finally understand that although I may have found the "right" way when it comes to lots of things like food waste, budgeting, time management, and organization, it was the absolute wrong way for me. The pressure to maintain the right way was exhausting, making me impatient with the ones I love and taking precious time away from the work I have to do in this world.

Shadows.

My opinion used to be as clear and sharp as the shadows from the
     noonday sun.
A crisp, clean line between what was dark and what was light, leaving
     little to be pondered.

I would draw my barrier around anything that could suck me into the
     darkness, living only for the light.
And once someone stepped into the shadows, they were too gone to be
     seen in the right.

It felt so easy, and it felt so clear—you're either wrong in your opinion
     or you are over here—
On the light side of things.

Yet, the funny thing about the sun at noon, the shadows don't stay in
one place for long.
And as we make our way around the sun, the light dances and fades
and shifts, and there is less guarantee of which side you are on.

And I think that's how it's been for me to grow. The clear, distinct lines
have all started to look like shadow.

Less cut and clear and more shades of gray.
What used to feel obviously right has started to look just OK, and the
things I would judge from my place in the sun all of the sudden
make sense when you consider the desperation that comes from
being left out in the cold.

When you fall.

This afternoon I watched the skateboarders at Venice Beach.
My eyes locked on one who seemed to be in his element.
He flowed and flipped and stopped like he'd learned to roll before
he walked.

I was transfixed with the way every move seemed so precise, yet he
made it look easy.
I wasn't alone either—there were dozens of us all watching him
at once.
Until he fell.

He must have done hundreds of perfect flips that day, but this one took
  him down.
And he walked off the park like I did after my first slow dance—
Arms held to the side hoping that, somehow, he'd become invisible.

And I thought—that's how it feels to be told you messed up when
  you're trying with every fiber of your being to do something
  perfectly.
Like there's an audience there following your every move and then—
  boom—you fall.
You say one word too many, leave a typo in that note, or miss an
  appointment you thought you'd written down—and there you are,
  veins hot and heavy like they're full of molten lead.

On good days that moment is temporary.
Sure, the heaviness comes but it also goes
And life reenters your cheeks as your mind continues to flow.

But on the worst days it can feel like a scream of a replay
Going over and over the same old moment.
And it doesn't matter how many things you did right that day
The sensation of one going wrong sends your mind into a pit of
  questions—

"What if I was a fool to think myself worthy?"
"What if I am nothing special after all?"
"What if I am really asking for too much out of life?"

All of this exists because we hold the ultimate question at the core
of our being—"Can you be at once good and flawed, or do my
mistakes take away all of the good that I have done?"

And I think that's where it's helpful to remember our skateboarding
friend.
His hundredth flip that day bruised his knees and then his ego
But not a single one of us would say that his other ninety-nine perfect
flips were all a wash.
He was great at his craft—
And he fell.
The audience was rooting for him to get up and keep going, perhaps
even more than they were when he seemed without flaw.

And it's helpful to remember that there were probably thousands of
falls before that which brought him to this point, where I stood
shoulder to shoulder with others in awe of what he's done.
In fact, for him and, I think, for us too, there is no goodness without
flaw.
Our obsession with perfection limits our access to the potential
available to us when we are fully who we are.
So the next time our veins feel hot with lava and our heart sinks down
to our toes, maybe we can remember to root for ourselves to get
back up again, as we have done a thousand times before.

Sacred.

What if you were born sacred?
What if your goodness doesn't have to boil from your sweat and
    your tears?

What if there is nothing wrong with you,
And that which you thought you lacked was simply a place where love
    could go?

Sending love into your anger.
Love into your fear.
Love into your shame.

What if you weren't a project to be tinkered with but a human of flesh
    and bone simply meant to be tended to?

What if we traded in our constant fixing for nurturing and curiosity?

What are the needs that aren't being met?
The wounds that are yet to heal?
Where are the blisters that love can soothe?

How would it feel to say over yourself,

"I am here for myself in all my sacred glory and my needs, and my hurt
and my joys are not too much—they're just enough. I will hold love
over the parts that are too tender to share and breathe life into the
essence of what it means to simply be

Just

Right

As I am"?

A field guide to killing fun.

I have found the secret to killing fun.
I learned it on the road somewhere between having to grow up too soon
and feeling shame for experiencing pleasure.
You would think this is a skill I would try not to use, but I have found it
comes in handy when I am out of my element.
The secret to killing fun is as simple as trying to decide if this is
something that's fun for you.
Putting an experience under a microscope is an incredible way to
overcomplicate the sensation of joy.
Take a simple trip to the park, for example.
Do I like the way my feet feel in the wet grass?
Does it matter to me that I saw someone litter—is it my job to speak up
for the environment in this moment?

What are the ethics of parks, anyway? Do we really cut back perfectly beautiful forests, manicure them, and pave pathways just so humans will enjoy them more? Isn't that the very problem with humanity? Our destruction of something perfect just to have something more palatable?

That's a completely different trip to the park than one where we are simply there for the moment.

Feet blending with the earth, children laughing, the sound of water flowing, a brief moment of weightlessness on the swing. Eyes closed, head tilted up, embracing the warmth of the sun on our skin.

In some ways I have learned to live life like the first trip to the park. What is right, what is wrong, and what is OK to enjoy?

Relationships get analyzed as thoroughly as my income taxes. What could be improved? Where could we cut back? What do we need more of? Is this a good relationship or is it a bad relationship? Can I live with their habit of putting a dirty knife on the edge of the sink for the rest of my life?

These are questions that always get answered over time, whether we try to figure them out or not. Yet, the time spent attempting to figure them out is time we are not allowed to feel the joy of whatever is. When we put ourselves into the position of decider. We take ourselves out of the role of enjoyer. Through this practice of weighing out our options, we eliminate our chance to be fulfilled.

Yet there's something within each of us that says there's only a certain amount of fun we're supposed to have—an internal glass ceiling that caps us off at a certain level of joy. And like that scene in *Willy Wonka and the Chocolate Factory,* where Charlie and his grandpa are floating to the roof, we imagine that we will be met with blades if we allow ourselves too much pleasure. So we find creative ways to belch our way down, making sure we stay where we think we're allowed.

But . . . what if we're meant to be in the elevator, bursting through in a glorious display of happiness with the ceiling falling away like fireworks? What if there was never too much good that you're allowed to feel, and no punishment is waiting on the other side of pleasure?

What if you could trust yourself to be good, even when your enjoyment takes a front seat?

Stone.

You are stone steady—
Each line a thoughtful gesture—
Each step an intentional stroll.

The phrase "work first, play second" is woven into the clenching of
    your jaw.

And with all of the improving that there is to do, you—
Wrap your fist around "perfection doesn't exist, but we should all try to
    be excellent."
Like there is ever an end to better.

And I can feel the heat rise in your cheeks when you think that you've
    been frivolous.
Like there is shame in purposeless joy.

And I wonder when you miss some sleep if you try to catch it later—
    because I fear you've not quite learned to rest.
Tossing aside the fruits of your labor as you continue to be your best.

Do you fear that you'll get off too easy when you get carried away
    in fun?
Or is it simply that you're focused on just one more thing to be done?

Finally resting.

When I was practicing yoga at home, I used to skip Savasana, the final rest post. The moment where we get to lie down and enjoy the benefits of all that we'd worked for. This was the part that felt dispensable to me. Like it was just an unnecessary element that could easily be skipped over.

It's ironic that it's also the way I've lived a majority of my life—skipping the parts where I enjoy the fruits of my labor in favor of finding the next thing that I should and could be focusing on.

Last week, I was hit with a surprising week of sickness, and this week, I'm still managing recovery. There's an inner struggle that occurs, a fear that I'm taking it too easy. That I'm enjoying my rest a little too much. That there's something I SHOULD be doing instead of healing.

I was continuously reminded last week, and yet again this morning, that this is what we've worked for. This is why I work so hard. So that the days in which I can't quite show up, everything doesn't fall apart.

Vacations, sick days, time off—this is our lived Savasana. Our chance to integrate all of the hard work that we've been doing. The chance to feel the fruits of our labor.

Resting was always OK.

Listening to not just our bodies when they demand that we rest but also to our hearts when they're overburdened, our minds when they're scattered, and our souls when they feel lost for inspiration.

Rest is not only OK but it's almost always the answer.

Everything sucks.

Once someone gave me the advice that
Everything sucks.
Every job sucks.
Every marriage sucks.
In its own way, everything sucks.

At first, this was upsetting to me.
"Who stole your rose-colored glasses?" I thought. But over the years it
    has been a comfort.
Remembering that perfection doesn't exist.
That everything will be beautiful, and it will also be terrible at times.

The trouble is expecting one much more than the other.
Expecting the terrible means never believing for more, numbing to the
    hope of the universe.

Expecting perfection means never being satisfied—comparing yours
to theirs.
A life lived in black and white, missing all the deep colors of the
in-between.

And one day after months of seeking perfection—
I woke up bored with my lack of appreciation.
And just like that it was time to fall in love with life again.

Rosie.

Some of my darkest moments have been the result of letting discipline
take over so much that there is no window left open for inspiration.

A tireless pursuit only matters if I am working toward something of
meaning.
A lesson learned over and over like a child needing to be reminded not
to touch the hot stove.

My mother, she calls me Rosie,
A nickname that flows so effortlessly
And is so full of love that it often feels more like my true name.

"Rosie, everything will be OK."
"Rosie, you're doing great."
"Rosie, I know you're busy, but I'd love to see you any day."

When I'm in the rhythm of producing for productions' sake, I can't see
Rosie anymore.
The playfulness of childhood, the innocence of believing that all will be
OK, I have buried them in the dirt floor of my childhood fort.

To forget how it feels to be Rosie means
Being a writer with nothing to say
A photographer with a broken trigger finger
And a mother who has lost her compassion.

Rosie is scared of exhaustion.
She shyly hides behind my skirt when she looks at a week full of
meetings
And she cries out for mercy when I ignore her begging for a break.

She loves the morning time, birdsong, and candlelight.
She dances boldly when seeing a new city for the first time
And feels safe with her hands in the dirt tending to the garden.

When Rosie is in charge, I am happy even when life is hard
Because she knows how to make the most out of any situation.
I am so full to the brim with ideas that I can't help but write them and
We dance, and we sing, and we play.

I am learning to let her lead more
To trust in her childlike wisdom
And to echo the words of my mother back into
Her heart, "Rosie, you can do anything, and I am so happy you
are here."

CONCLUSION

To the part in all of us that feels they must be above reproach.

There's a video of me as a child swinging on a tire swing we'd hung in our front yard.

The swing was made of tattered rope, and I clung to it for dear life—my five-year-old hands barely able to hang on.

My hair was wild and curly, my clothes tattered and worn. I was covered in dirt or maybe chocolate?

My brothers were pushing me higher and higher, and I laughed so loudly that it echoed in the valley where we lived.

I was a wild animal left to roam and to scream and to make messes all along the way.

Contrast that with the photograph of me dressed up for Easter. Every hair in place, a dress completely unruffled, shoes tied a bit too tight, and a perfect frown on my face. The same feeling followed me to the high school prom, where I spent hours putting myself together only to feel too stiff and uncomfortable to have a good time. A statue intended for the approval of other people's eyes left lonely and cold as the world kept on dancing.

I think that's what we do sometimes in life. We want to do the right thing or have things look the right way so much that we spend all of our energy in the fixing. We hyper-focus on the tiny details, getting each one in just the right spot. We cinch in our pleasures with discipline and structure to guarantee our place in heaven, and we squeeze our feet into shoes too tight hoping that we'll be steps ahead of those wishing to catch us off guard.

But, in all of that fixing and tinkering and being reformed, we miss out on the simple pleasures of life. The wild freedom that our childhood selves learned to silence somewhere along the way. The messy, the playful, and the free.

In each of us roars a lion-hearted child who is begging to spin in circles until they're dizzy and stomp around when they are tired. The part of us that knows it's OK to be angry and it's safe to make mistakes. The littlest voice still swinging somewhere in our gut waiting for us to stop being statues and start being us.

CHAPTER TWO

*

*To the part of you that fears
being unlovable.*

INTRODUCTION TO TYPE TWO

The Enneagram type two is commonly referred to as "the helper, giver, and lover." They are warm, loving, helpful, and flattering and fear being unlikeable or unlovable. This chapter is dedicated to the part in all of us that never quite feels worthy of love and the part that struggles to put ourselves first and believes our sacrifice is the price we pay for relationships. In this chapter, we will address complex elements related to the Enneagram type two structure, such as:

1. Giving what they hope to receive

Often our type twos have a blind spot when it comes to their own needs. They can be so focused on the needs of others that they forget to check in with what's going on with them. Because of this, they may find that they're often giving exactly what they hope to receive: throwing you the birthday they want you to throw for them, filling up your glass of water when they're thirsty, or even saying "thank you" as often as they'd like to receive appreciation.

2. Crossing the boundaries of others

Giving without being asked to give can be seen as a crossing of boundaries. That can take the form of unsolicited advice, invasive support, or grand gestures that create an inequitable relationship. This can leave the people in their life feeling invaded upon, while the type two wonders why no one appreciates them.

3. Fear of being unlovable

At the core of the type two structure is really just a human wanting to know that they are worthy of love—that they are enough to secure their relationships. The trouble is that they've learned to feel secure in their relationships by becoming indispensable, by showing up and being of service. This leaves them feeling uncertain as to whether they could be loved as they are and inevitably resentful of how much they sacrifice to "earn their place."

4. Dissatisfaction in relationships

A lot of type twos experience an undercurrent of dissatisfaction in their relationships. This can happen because they are so focused on giving and serving that they struggle to receive. They struggle to know what they need and if it's OK to ask for their needs to be met. They may feel as though the people in their life don't love them because they're looking for very specific signifiers of love that only they know about. The people in their life are expected to anticipate the needs of the type two and to essentially be mind readers.

5. Mistaking pity for love

At times, type twos may confuse being pitied for all of their sacrifices and exhaustion as a display of love. Because of this, when the type two needs to feel cared for, they will express their agony, their exhaustion, or their frustration with overextending themselves in hopes that people will empathize with them and share affection. It's a false signifier that they are cared for; instead, they are likely missing the real signs of love in their attempts to see themselves as sacrificial.

6. Overextending and lack of self-care

Many type twos traditionally feel as though there isn't enough time for themselves—that if they do take time to put themselves first, they are doing a selfish thing. It may feel shameful or difficult to say no, to set healthy boundaries, or even to just do the things they enjoy to do alone.

Although they were written with the type two structure in mind, these essays and poems are an invitation to explore the part in each of us that feels the need to earn our sense of belonging. My hope is that they give you more permission to take care of yourself, greater access to self-love, and an invitation to set healthy and loving boundaries with both yourself and others.

On self-love.

I started practicing yoga about ten years ago. I'd recently settled down into a small town in North Carolina and was yet to make adult friendships where I lived. I worked from home at the time and spent all day alone. So, as my way of connecting to something other than the closet I'd turned into my office—I signed up for a daily yoga class at the local community gym. It took place every day at noon, and I never missed a class.

My favorite part about this particular class was that I was the youngest person in the room. In fact, I was the only person under sixty that seemed to attend, and that was more than perfect for me. This class and these women, who never knew my name but became faces so familiar I can see them now when I close my eyes, were my respite from an otherwise lonely life. I was married to someone who didn't really seem to understand me and adjusting to a life of stillness in a small town. This was the one time of day where I didn't have to carry the burden of feeling lonely, even when I wasn't alone.

One particular afternoon, at the end of class, the teacher said, "Thank yourself for coming here today. For doing something good for your body and your mind."

And something inside of me clicked.

In that instant, the world seemed to shift and the tectonic plates of my heart moved a mile.

I had never in my life thanked myself for anything.

I'd been operating as though there was nothing of worth within me and any good thing I did or positive outcome from my actions were all somehow a fluke of nature or the doing of some all-knowing, all-judging higher power. Because of this, I let all appreciation ricochet off me like a BB hitting metal. The unconscious belief being that I was not worthy of thanks, and if I accepted it, then I would be even less worthy of it—anything good in me was not of me, and therefore, it wasn't mine to appreciate.

In that one moment, lying on my mat surrounded by strangers with familiar faces, I was invited into a new way of being. A sense that I made the choice to show up that day. That I chose each step that brought me to that exact moment.

Sure, showing up for a yoga class isn't curing cancer, but it is something. It is a small bit of good done for myself just to be happier and healthier and more connected.

And it was good, and I did that.

Years later, I sat with my current husband having morning coffee like we always do, and I told him of how hard I worked at that stage of my life. All of the hours put into growing a new photography business—all of the creative ways I'd figured out to pay the bills. I told him that I never felt like my ex-husband saw me. Like he didn't see how hard I was working and how dedicated and excited I was to making my own way. I would work holidays and weekends trying to build something out of nothing, and it was like he only saw the lack.

I guess for years I waited for someone to see me, someone to say thank you for everything you're doing for yourself and for us.

But that opening in my heart—created in what may have been a seniors' yoga class at the Waynesville Recreation Center in 2011—taught me that there is no need to wait for someone else to see all that you are doing. You can create that for yourself. So I learned to tell myself "thank you."

Almost a decade and a whole marriage later, I was up at 2 a.m. with my crying stepson, singing him an out-of-tune lullaby as he struggled to fall asleep. And the desire for someone to see me arose again. A hope that someone, anyone, would notice all that I was giving. And I took that moment to practice a lesson from so many years before. I put a hand on my heart and thought to myself, "Thank you for all that you are doing. Thank you for loving this kid so well. I am so proud of you for showing up like this even when your efforts aren't seen. You are doing a great job."

Oddly enough, my current husband is a waterfall of kind words, a poet at making me feel seen and loved and celebrated. He is the embodiment of a supportive husband, and yet, I still ache for reassurance at times when he's not available or, even more likely, when his reassurance isn't enough to quench the thirst of my childhood wounds.

A funny thing happens when we learn to show love to ourselves in these ways—we stop begging for scraps from those around us, and we learn to recognize those who can love us where we are. We are drawn to the reassuring, the compassionate, and the giving. We are no longer seeking out those in need hoping we can give them enough in order to finally be worthy of love.

And just like the tomatoes.

Today, I am trying to remember that—just like the tomatoes
Need to come inside when the nights are too cold—
I can also allow myself a place of comfort when all feels lost.

And just like when I prune off the dead leaves to give the plant more
   energy for the ones that are still working—
I can focus my attention on the areas that are going well and eliminate
   the things that suck the life out of me.

And as I water their soil and put them in the sun,
I can remember to tend to my own needs with the same
Amount of attention and concern.

And although I may not wither visibly upon neglect,
I do know how it feels to be a flower ready to turn to fruit only to find
   that I am without what I need to move forward.

So, as I pause to inspect the leaves and tend to the soil—

I am reminded to also pay close attention to the things that make me
grow and the ones that leave me dormant.

To the one who suffers most.

I think a lot about that scene in *Titanic* where Rose is laid out like a star
across a queen-sized door while Jack grasps onto the side, frozen and
sinking. We could all see that there was plenty of door to go around, and
our humanity screamed that his sacrifice was just a little bit—

Extra.

Just like I believe Jack and Rose could have found a way for both of
them to survive, I believe it's actually pretty rare and unusual to have to
ration out good things.

We may not have an abundance to share, but, in general, there is
usually enough for each of us to have some. Rose may have had to squeeze
herself to the side of the door for Jack to fit—neither of them getting an
abundance of door—but both would've made it out alive. Similarly, in life,
there is usually one small sacrifice from each of us that can guarantee we
are all taken care of.

So why is it that you believe the one who suffers most is allowed to
have their needs met?

Like only the one who is thirsty gets a drink even though there is water
enough for all of us?

And how many times do you go without unnecessarily in order for
others to float?

And even more so—how many times have you thought that your suffering was the only way to be seen in your need?

I can see how the belief that goods are rationed to those who need them most would lead you to think that if you are too happy no one would take care of you.

So often we confuse pity for love, causing us to look for the desperation in the eyes of those seated across from us.

If they need so much, then we must give and give until we are bone dry.

And unless we are bone dry, we do not deserve a drink of water because there is always someone thirstier.

But what if you deserved to have your needs met even when you're well nourished?

Even when you are rested?

What if, even in your abundance, you can ask for more?

What if suffering is not the currency you have to exchange for love?

The art of self-forgetting.

How do you recognize your own voice after days of self-forgetting?

It's almost like romanticizing the idea of not existing.

Exchanging yourself for the roles you play in relationships.

The perfect parent, worker, or friend.

Calling it love when, really, it's self-abandonment.

The phrase, "How can I help?"

Taking place of the much truer—too vulnerable—"Where do I fit in?"

I don't mean to sound harsh—I just want to be clear.

Because watching you funnel all your love out while hoping someone
will notice you're on empty, feels like watching someone smoke
while hooked up to an oxygen tank.
You have the love you need; you just keep giving it away.

Tiny anvils.

I have often held on to the illusion that I could be a part of everyone's
solution. Like, if I just pushed or wished or helped hard enough, then we
could all be the best versions of ourselves—
Together!
The trouble with this logic is that it rarely actually helps anyone. In
fact, no one even knows I'm doing it, but I carry around the heaviness of the
burden as if it's mine to bear. The idea that people are not able to handle
their situations without my intervention is ridiculous. They've all been fine
before me, and they will all be fine after me. Yet somehow, I fear that things
will blow up if I don't intervene.
What this looks like is carrying around little anvils of other people's
problems that they never even asked for me to hold. The only person
negatively impacted is me. I'm collecting burden after burden and gripping
tighter and tighter in hopes that it will makes things better, yet it only makes
me more tired and resentful and difficult to get along with.
It's funny because I have all these goals and dreams. Goals to liberate
women from boring lives where we are trained to settle, goals to participate
actively and passionately in the pursuit of equality for all people, goals
to love my people and see the world. Yet, instead of giving my undivided

energy to these things, I collect anvil after anvil of other people's struggles and goals and dreams as if they are my own.

It's not like they like it either; they don't. They want to be loved for where they are now, and that's ultimately my only job. Yet, I think they need to thrive according to my standards of what that means, and I power through to make that happen FOR them—against their will sometimes.

I started doing this meditation where I imagine cutting them off like balloons. Each balloon is an outcome, a person, or a situation I'd like to control. Some are light and floaty, and others feel like lead. I envision myself carrying all these problems and situations that are 100 percent out of my control, and I laugh at myself for falling victim to this mind trickery. Then, I take each one, mindfully cut it off, and watch it either float away or sink.

What is left is what I can actually impact—myself and myself alone.

And she looks so much lighter there without the weight of the world tied to her shoulders, and she looks like she has so much space for more of what she actually wants to be giving her energy to. In that moment—I'm happy for her.

Aggressively helpful.

There's this coffee shop across the street from my office that has become my chosen place for self-care. It's beautiful, has great coffee, and they have the prettiest glassware. So, when the earth feels like it's moving beneath my feet or my responsibilities have me in a choke hold, I will take a good book to the café, grab an espresso in a fancy glass, and just give myself a moment to breathe.

One afternoon a few weeks ago, I walked in and there were several tables with dishes that customers hadn't put away. Before I even realized what I was doing, I'd already bussed two tables for them. On my way to the third, I realized I was doing it again—that thing where I play the savior.

I see a need, and I take it upon myself to be the solution, whether anyone asked for it or not.

The problem is that needs are everywhere you look, and sometimes it's just not your place to fix them. In this particular circumstance, I was thrashing and drowning in my own turbulent waters trying to do someone else's job for them. Other times, I take on people's problems as if they're my own, stepping in to try to save the day—bulldozing over their boundaries—and feeling frustrated when they don't take my completely unsolicited advice.

This tendency bleeds into my friendships, and I've surrounded myself with other folks seeking to be of service. In fact, I have a good friend who refers to himself as "aggressively helpful." Being friends with him is amazing because he is such a great support and one of my biggest cheerleaders. But it took me years to realize that unless I was just as aggressively helpful with him, we'd be in a very uneven dynamic. So, I became aggressively helpful in response, or at least aggressively questioning of him every time he offers to help: "Do you really want to give me your Nespresso machine, or do you need to ask me to pay for it?" I'm sure there are times where things are uneven, but I am aggressively skeptical of his giving so he knows he can take it back whenever he needs. Between the two of us, we've worked hard to find a healthy balance between offering support and over-sacrificing. And I think this only works because we're both terrified of taking too much. Our particular neuroses are beautifully aligned. But what happens when we point this loving energy in the direction of people without our particular set of quirks?

I think the term "aggressive" is very appropriate here, because that's the difference between being supportive and thinking that we're saving people. It's not our place to aggressively look for opportunities to be the solution to other people's problems. However, we can be lovingly supportive and available when we are asked.

I learned this lesson at an Enterprise Rent-A-Car at LAX. I'd been traveling for twelve hours already and was feeling sleepy and disoriented. The woman who showed me to my car was very concerned that I wouldn't have enough room in the trunk for my luggage and was taking it upon herself to put it in the car for me. The trouble is that I had things I needed to get out of my suitcase and a preference as to how I would organize my car. In a way, her attempts to help were actually causing me more stress.

That's the tricky thing with being aggressively helpful. It's guessing at what you think someone else may need, instead of waiting for them to tell you if they need anything at all. It relies on you doing what YOU would want in that situation and not taking the individual in front of you into account.

It's like when my kid wants a cookie—he always asks for one by saying, "Hey, Sarajane, do YOU want a cookie?"

Not, "Can I have a cookie?"

Not just walking into the kitchen and grabbing one—consequences be damned.

It's, "Sarajane, do YOU want a cookie?"

I used to think, "Do I look like I want a cookie or something? What is going on?"

Until one afternoon, I realized that HE wanted a cookie. It's just easier for him not to feel rejected if he asks me if I would like one instead. It's easier to swallow than the outright "no" he's afraid of receiving by asking if HE can have one.

I think that's a good thing to remember. When we find ourselves wanting to play God—to take on the role of fixer—in reality, this is just information about what we want or would want in the same situation. It's all a projection of our own desires.

WE want the luggage loaded into our car. WE want friends who give without expecting payment in return. WE want someone to buy us lunch for once.

WE want the cookie.

The giving tree.

Have you mourned the loss of self that comes with being all things to
all people?
The slivers of you that get severed as you meet everyone where
they are?
And isn't it heavy when your love is like molasses?
Steady and sticky and strong. Pouring outward from you like a tree
trunk dried.

And how many times have you made yourself breathless and
exhausted—
Filling their cup with emotional water to the point of overflowing while
you are thirsty?

And are your eyes tired from scanning as you look for proof that they
    couldn't live without you?
Because they whispered to me in that moment where your smile didn't
    quite reach your lashes, and I wonder
If they could use a rest.

And I know you fear you won't be loved if you stop letting them borrow
    from your branches—
But even the strongest trees can't shade us when they're gone.

Temporary tattoos.

I used to think my worth could be negotiated.
That goodness and identity were bottled and sold
On whatever shelf people found their belonging.

Each word someone shared
About who they thought I was,
Got painted onto my skin.
And for years, I thought they were tattoos
Only to realize that they wash right off with
Water and a little self-respect.

And it turns out, worth isn't up for debate
And I get to choose the words I'd tattoo on my skin—
Brave.

Kind.
Passionate.

And I read them to myself every morning
Through blood and tears as I wrestled with my
Infinite worth.
I read them through gritted teeth on days I believed them
And on days that I did not. I read them and I chose the voices that
echoed
Them back to me to remain in my life.
I toiled with my demons and fought for my soul—until people started
asking me which shelf
I got my confidence from.

Feeling unloved.

Lately, it feels like a string is tied to my heart—and with each strained
interaction someone yanks it with all they've got.
My eyes become aqueducts and my stomach a hurricane.

This sensation is so brutally undesirable that I jump into action at any
slight hint that it could arise.
Just let everything be OK. Let's just all be OK.

My throat burns from holding back the screams of, "I don't think
anyone loves me."

As I worry about whether they've eaten enough for lunch or how they
will get enough sleep tonight.

So, I busy myself trying to sew up the holes in the fabric of our
connections by managing our schedule, keeping the dishes
washed, and giving them all of my attention.

And then I seethe.

Anger boiling in my chest as I scrub one more tomato soup stain off the
godforsaken counter

And

"I DON'T THINK ANYONE LOVES ME!"

Boils in my veins.

And I think, "I'm not grateful enough for what I have."

And try to fix it all within myself.
If I could just be happy, then everything will be OK. We will all just
be OK.

They need to eat.
They need to sleep.

They need me to be happy to see them after a day of bleeding myself
out where the tomato stains used to lie on the counter.

I just want someone to love me.

A partner's perspective.

Lately it feels like nothing I do is enough—
Every bid to show affection is dismissed and
I'm afraid I'm foolish if I don't give up.

This sensation is so brutally undesirable that I hesitate to make grand
gestures out of fear that they'll be missed.
I just want you to be OK. Let's just all be OK.

My eyes sting from the way you let the words "I love you" pass by as
though they've not been said. Your eyes darting toward the next
thing that needs to be taken care of.

You're so focused on whether I've eaten or slept that you don't have
time to really connect.

I cleaned the bathroom today hoping you would notice, but you were
so busy making sure I didn't have to take care of myself that it felt
like a drop in the bucket.

And then I pull back.

You looked incredible this morning as you got ready for the day, and I
put my arms around you to whisper compliments in your ear, but
the words were shrugged off with a self-effacing comment, and my
arms unlinked from your waist as you rushed to do the dishes.

And I want to scream,

"DON'T YOU SEE HOW MUCH I LOVE YOU!"

It's like I'm playing a game of twenty questions—
Which gesture of love will be enough today?

Sometimes you need to hear the words—
Other times it's touch that you crave.
Some days I know you just want me to wash the tomato soup off the
counter, but I always seem to be off—the right gesture at the
wrong time.

I just want you to know that I love you.
I love you.
I LOVE YOU!

CONCLUSION

To the part in all of us that feels they must save others.

I can remember vividly the moment I first saw my mother cry. She'd gone away to her bedroom, and I opened the door to find her lying under the covers with tears in her eyes. We talked of her worries and the burdens she was carrying, and I felt uneasy.

Part of me wanted to lay a healing hand on her heart and tell her it's going to be all right, and another part just wanted it to stop.

She was the foundation for me—the very thing I'd built my life on—and if she was shaking, my world might fall apart.

I'm not saying that it started there, but I do know I spent years of my life believing that I would save my mother. Instead of worrying if her foundation was solid, I would become the foundation myself. One day, I would win the lottery and buy her a house. One day, I would take all of her pain away.

She never asked me to take that burden onto myself, but I felt her suffering, and I wanted to end it for her.

As I got older, I came to understand that I was so focused on her pain, I'd been completely neglecting my own. It was close to a decade of being an adult before I started to truly grieve the childhood I didn't have. To understand the ways I grew up too fast by trying to fill the gaps to guarantee that no one ever fell through.

When I was nine years old, I stood in the kitchen as my mother taught me how to suck in my stomach, so I looked thinner. She signed me up for Weight Watchers that same week. I would be her accountability buddy.

I learned at that time to ignore my hunger cues, to fear food. My job was to be as little as possible and not to enjoy the act of eating.

I started going for jogs on the dirt road where our trailer was located and weighing myself every day.

Later in high school, on my third attempt at this diet, I found that I could lose weight if I only ate unbuttered popcorn and drank Diet Coke. Eventually, the hunger would go away if I let my stomach growl enough. Others at the meetings saying that it starts to feel good when your stomach growls, like it's eating the fat away.

I believed that if I could just be everything that my family needed me to be, then we'd all be OK. I would be the one thing my mother didn't have to worry about, and she would love me because I earned it through my sacrifice and my hunger, through hard work, and not asking for too much when she was already doing enough.

I would help not burden her.

So just like I learned to ignore my hunger cues, I learned to alter my experience with need in general. If I tried hard enough, I felt I could will myself not to need anything from anyone. I would be the last thing anyone had to worry about.

These things have their time limits though. We all have to eat, and we all have to feel loved. So, like a beautifully fluffy stomach shoved into jeans too small, instead of focusing on making the stomach thinner, I learned that it's OK to just buy her a new pair of jeans and let the lady rest.

We are not loved for our sacrifice. We are not loved for our ability to go without. We do not need to go empty and feel the rumbling growl of a life left wanting because we're afraid of asking for too much.

CHAPTER THREE

*

*To the part of you that feels you are
only as worthy as your achievements.*

INTRODUCTION TO TYPE THREE

The Enneagram type three is commonly referred to as "the achiever" or "performer." They are efficient, goal-oriented, and motivated to succeed. This chapter is dedicated to the part in all of us that feels we must be successful in order to be worthy. The part that forgets that life is not all about productivity and worries about how we appear to others. In this chapter, we will address complex elements related to the Enneagram type three structure, such as:

1. Struggling with comparison

When the focus of attention is on being the best, everyone becomes your competition. Type threes can begin to see people as competitors, watching the people in their life to see if they have more and wanting to make sure they keep up. Keeping an eye on those in their industry to make sure they aren't doing better than the type three. At times, the type three roots for their competitors to fail out of fear that they will outshine them if they don't. The healthiest type threes I know have come to terms with this impulse and make something good out of it, finding ways to embrace community and resist competition.

2. Confusing admiration for love

Many type threes are seeking out the next acknowledgment of how much they've achieved. Performing for the eyes of those who are going to be impressed with them. This can leave them motivated when there's something to gain and unmotivated when no one is watching. They often need to find a sense of connection to their work and goals that go beyond other people so that they are excited to participate even when not acknowledged. This can also go into their relationships—being the perfect spouse or child so that their partner admires them but forgetting to connect on a deeper, more vulnerable level where they can be loved for who they are and not what they do.

3. Grappling with imposter syndrome

Imposter syndrome is defined as, "The persistent inability to believe that one's success is deserved or has been legitimately achieved as a result of one's own efforts or skills." This can show up for our type threes in a couple of ways: When we focus on success as a goal, we find that we are constantly moving the target. Once one goal is accomplished, the stakes get higher, the goalpost moves, and there is always more to be done. There is never an end to what can be accomplished, and therefore, there is never a sense of having "made it." Additionally, many type threes prioritize the appearance of success over actual success, causing them to cut corners, fib about their accomplishments, or even go into crippling debt. This can leave them looking successful but feeling like a failure inside. The remedy to both of these is a fun mixture of authenticity and feelings-based goals—choosing a lifestyle that they want to live versus goals they want to achieve, and being open about their successes and their failures so they can be seen and accepted for the truth of who they are.

4. Being the golden child

For many type threes, their family of origin had one or several of the following scenarios—there was an immense amount of pressure to be successful from their family of origin, their parents worked hard for them to have opportunities that the parents didn't have, or they wanted to make sure they didn't end up in the same situation as the rest of their family. Maybe they grew up poor and wanted to make sure they never wanted for anything again. Maybe they come from a family of addiction and want to end that cycle. Many type threes I've met are first-generation Americans who feel pressure to make their parents' sacrifices mean something. In other scenarios, they come from a family of high achievers, and they are just trying to keep up. No matter the reason, they all felt the pressure to be the best—a shining example of success.

5. Pushing their feelings aside to get the job done

Many type threes are able to push their feelings off until later, setting them aside to get the job done. The trouble is they may lose touch with who they are, what they truly want, and the pain that comes from some of their less helpful behaviors. Once a type three is able to be really honest with themselves and others about how they are feeling and what they want, they are able to build a life that is truly fulfilling for them, but this is only possible if they let their feelings have a voice at the table.

6. Confronting image consciousness

If appearing successful is your main motivation and failure feels like the way to lose connection, then you are inevitably going to be concerned about how others view you. Type threes typically have a specific image they want to portray. They tend to hide the darker parts of themselves as well as their failures. They may cultivate an image or a brand that feels separate from who they truly are. It's imperative that type threes have at least one or two people who know them deep, deep down so they can rest without having to perform. The thing that often stands in the way of this is their fear of being seen as someone who needs help as opposed to being the one others can look to for inspiration.

Although they were written with the type three structure in mind, these essays and poems are an invitation to explore the part in each of us that feels we must succeed at all costs. My hope is that they give you permission to define success on your own terms, freedom to rest, and openness to being supported in your most vulnerable positions.

Mastering vulnerability.

I learned my first lesson of vulnerability at two o'clock in the morning in a North Carolina diner.

I'd committed to volunteer at a weekend event and couldn't afford the gas to get myself home and back.

I also couldn't afford food.

I was too afraid to sleep in my car and too embarrassed to tell anyone.

So I determined I would just stay up all night doing homework at Waffle House.

I ordered a one-dollar cup of coffee that provided me infinite refills and real estate.

I can still remember the way my eyes burned from forcing them to stay open and my nose and the back of my jaw from holding back tears.

Later that night, a few acquaintances of mine came in for a late-night meal and joined me at my table. They were curious about my weird choice to be there alone, wondered where my parents were, and why I wouldn't order food with them.

I didn't want to be seen as someone who needed help. As someone who didn't have her life together. I didn't want to be so obviously in need of accolades that I would put myself through this for a volunteer opportunity.

With hot, burning cheeks I told them the truth.

And they helped.

They ordered me food, filled up my tank, and gave me a place to sleep for the night.

And they never mentioned it again.

I was so scared to be seen in my weakness, but that moment of putting down my mask allowed me to feel supported by people I was keeping at arm's length.

Years before, I was in the church lobby when a pastor called me into his office and told me that he'd be paying our power bill that month and asked if I had enough money for groceries.

I was in the gas station as my mother told the attendant of my stepfather's latest relapse, and my cheeks flushed as the attendant put the gas on her tab once again.

I was a teenager whose family friends took the time to help me buy school clothes for the coming season.

I sat in my living room—my mom having beers with friends talking of their interactions with bill collectors. They laughed at the oddity of calling people without money telling them to give you money but knowing that there wasn't money to give. The husband told a story of a question he asked a debt collector:

"Are you worried about whether I pay this or not?"

"Yes, sir, I am very worried about this."

"Well, there's no need in both of us being worried then."

And my mom's friend hung up.

At thirty-five—I am yet to feel the freedom and joy they held in that moment, the ease of laughing at their situation and their acceptance of each other in what could feel like a shameful situation.

I'm reminded of my own private experiences with bill collectors and missing payments. My silent suffering while I tried to maintain appearances. The suffering is the same—but I did it alone.

These moments embarrassed me. I felt ashamed that we were in need and wanted to hide on the floorboard of the car when the truth of our situation came to light.

Yet, my mother had mastered vulnerability. Admitting her limitations and honoring her weakness. Because of that, we were showered with support from our community. Human angels poured into our family, and we were not alone.

And this is the reminder to all of us who feel the need to seem like we have it all together.

The walls we build to hide our failings are begging for us to at least open a window and let love flow in.

When we are seen and loved—even at our weakest—

It is in those moments and perhaps those alone where we can truly know that we are loved not for what we do but instead for who we are.

Are the azaleas OK?

The azaleas have started to bloom
And their bright-pink petals are breathtaking
Against the green backdrop of spring.

I can't help but wonder how it feels for them in winter.
Do they forget how beautiful they are when we are no longer stopping
    to admire them?
Do they appreciate the privacy of blending into the background?

Do they feel confident that they'll bloom again, or
Do they lose hope like us creatives when the chill sets in?

On feeling.

I have a switch that I flip in my brain that turns off my feelings. If a feeling is particularly inconvenient or overwhelming, I will often flip the switch. Flipping the switch feels like relegating that thought to one barricaded area of my brain so that I can focus my energy on other things. Sometimes the energy feels frenetic, and I become stressed as I try to do thirty things at once. Sometimes it's finding fun things to do or watching videos of places I plan to travel to as a mental escape. It almost always sounds like, "I can't talk/think/write about that right now because I have _ _ _ _ to do."

Yesterday, I flipped the switch. It was a day that I had a lot of work to get done and videos to record, and I didn't want to be puffy on camera or take too long to finish my tasks. I sat down in the morning with my journal and began to answer the prompt I've answered daily since my father took his life—"What are three things that you are grieving today?" And I didn't have access to them. I could THINK of them—my mind running with concepts and ideas of feelings—but I couldn't FEEL them. Nothing moved in my heart.

In this season, my husband has been asking me to discuss my feelings nightly, and last night—my hands gripped around a pillow serving as armor for my gut—I told him that I struggled to feel them and how going deeper felt like more tears and more headaches and more sadness and that it just feels so inconvenient. He simply said, "I think you're going to have to get used to sadness being a part of your daily life." I've been trying to compartmentalize my feelings: taking time off of work to feel, going on a road trip to the deep south as a way to feel things alone, waiting until the end of the day to let myself feel things once the work is done.

The idea of integrating sadness into my daily life goes against every tactic I've learned for success. It means learning and unlearning what being a business owner, a parent, and a wife means when it's not powering up and getting things done.

It's inviting a conversation with the truth of who I am to the table every single morning and bringing that wholeness into my schedule each day.

At the altar.

I've spent my time worshipping at the altar of productivity.
Melting away my moments into streams of checks on a list of things
    to do.

I've optimized the roles I play at work and at home, and I do it all with a
    can-do attitude.

So, why do I feel so sad?

I have learned to ride the high of my achievements.
The feeling of success coursing through my veins until

Darkness hits again.

The new becomes normal and I am left alone and more desperate than
    before looking everywhere to

Get

My

Next

Fix.

And as the achievements get bigger, the stakes get higher, and the
   feelings just aren't flowing anymore.

All of the sudden there is more to lose.

Less to gain.
But,
"I DID EVERYTHING THEY TOLD ME TO DO!"
I picked a path and went all in.
I jumped on the escalator and rode it

All

The

Way

To

The

Top.

This isn't what they said it would feel like.
I thought there'd be a moment where peace was earned.
Where I felt like I could finally turn off.

But each new level needs more and more from me.
A never-ending changing of gears.

I'm afraid if I don't decide to get off the ride cold turkey
I'll find myself locked in a corner office—microdosing my emotions so I
    can make it to the weekend.

Where I wait comatose and wanting until another week begins.

The philosophy of choice.

For most of my life, I've lived by the philosophy, "If you don't like something, either change it or accept it." The idea that everything in my life is a choice. I either chose the circumstance, or I'm choosing to live with the circumstance, and I'm definitely choosing HOW I live in the circumstance.

Grief—when I was finally able to accept it—told me that I was spending all of this time using the philosophy of choice as a way to avoid the grief that already existed. The inherent sorrow of circumstances you can't control. To choose my feelings even though sometimes you just need to feel the ones that are there.

As Toni Morrison wrote, "It's just as sad as it ought to be and I'm not going to hide from what's true just because it hurts."

Many of us experienced this at the start of 2020—with the launching point of a pandemic. Our great teacher in being out of control. Sure, I can choose HOW I tell myself to feel about the year, but often that's at the expense of feeling the truth of what is there. The anger at injustice, the fear of the unknown, the disappointment with disregard for human life. There's a precious dance here. One that I am learning to find sacred. A giving in to my grief, an allowing of the truth of my body, taking right action in the direction of better circumstances for us all AND a release of the expectation that things need to BE good in order for me to FEEL good.

On quitting.

We're taught from a young age never to give up, as if letting go of something is comparative to stealing from your local grocery store.

Phrases on the walls of our school gymnasiums seemingly yelling in their bright-yellow lettering—

"Keep going!"

"Just do it!"

"Never say can't."

I wonder if the person who hung up those signs has ever felt the sweet ecstasy of saying, "Actually, I can't do this right now"?

That delightful moment where you cut the cord and let the thing that is overwhelming you fall away, leaving you full of blissful relief.

If we were honest about it, we would acknowledge that quitting is like getting a really good massage. A place where, for just a moment, everything is calm. Life is more open, and—if just for that instant—you are free.

I understand why we have these clichéd phrases. They're meant to push us past our comfort zone, not to give up before we succeed.

I'm reminded of a graphic I saw once of a man digging a tunnel underground, clearly exhausted and considering turning back. To him, the wall was the same as it had been for what we imagine were miles of digging, but what the viewer can see is that with just a few more strikes of the shovel, he'd have broken through to freedom. The message being— you never know how close you are to succeeding at the time you choose to give up.

It's like my husband's battle with shin splints last year. He loves to run, but as he was getting back into it, he would get these horrible shin splints. He'd take a few days to rest and then start again only to repeat the process.

After plenty of googling, he came to the answer—either you push through it and the shin splints will go away or you will permanently injure yourself. You won't know which one unless you try.

Pushing through could mean getting to the other side where you can experience more joy and a sense of accomplishment. Or pushing through could be taking away your chance to do this for the rest of your life.

Cool. Cool. Cool.

So how do you know when to call it quits and when to keep going? When will you simply heal through the pushing, and when will it take you past the point of no return?

And then there are times where it feels easy to quit and times where it feels impossible; how do we know which to trust?

Is it wrong to quit because we're fearful of letting our family down but then completely OK to move on if we know we're not going to succeed?

I think the fundamental truth we need to accept is that we are no less human because of what we left unaccomplished and no more worthy for what we do.

If we decide to push through and take the risk of loss in order to get where we hope to go, that's a choice we can make that could be rewarding.

Let's also remember, however, that success in the traditional sense isn't always the goal. Sometimes, success looks like knowing where to call your limits and allowing for life to be beautifully small.

Comparison.

Do you ever feel like you are running a race—heart pumping—eyes sharp on your competition?

Paying close attention to your neighbors, making sure you aren't left behind.

Keeping pace can feel exciting.

A reason to wake up in the morning.

An excuse to try harder than the day before.

Then there are those dangerous thoughts of hoping worse for those running beside you.

Feeling resentful of the times they pull ahead and unconsciously rooting for them to fail.

Like oil dropped into the ocean, feelings of competition leak into every part of our being until our thoughts go dark.

Those we are competing against aren't fazed because this was never about them anyway—instead it bleeds into *our* veins, and we boil from the inside out.

Turning our beautiful life into something we now take for granted because we want MORE.

Our accomplishments pale in comparison to something we've never done before.

And what happens when you realize you're exhausting yourself on a race that no one else signed up for? All of your so-called competitors are here just running for fun.

Enjoying the scenery, the wind on their skin—feeling the sun on their face.

While you glide beside them—trees in the distance blurry as you focus on winning and winning alone.

On following your heart.

I saw a vision of your heart today—
A nagging child pulling at your pant leg saying your name on repeat.

They wondered desperately why everything else seemed to be more important than what they had to say.

And I know you have dreams, and your ambitions feel like a lifeboat that will carry you to the place where you can finally pause long enough to listen.

But, I'm worried that by the time you get there, your heart will have lost the will to try.

Or

More likely, upon arriving at your destination, you will see the next one off in the distance, begging for one more leg of the journey to feel the way you thought you'd feel upon this arrival.

So, your weary arms keep rowing, never knowing when to stop because there is no resting place for those who find their worth in doing. There is only doing to be done.

And your heart is banging at the door of your chest, writhing with answers to what you really need, but choosing to listen means risking stagnation

And there are no gold stars for that.

Work is my favorite way to ignore the realities of life.

When I was in school, I used to make up homework assignments for myself. If the teacher hadn't sent anything home, I would come up with something. A random writing assignment no one asked for or multiplication sheets I'd write out myself. I'm not even sure I told anyone they weren't required. I honestly think I liked that they thought it was assigned to me.

Like I could disengage from the expectations at home if I had a lot of work to do.

I did the same thing with my first few businesses—making up work that could always be done. A new website every quarter. Assigning myself new platforms to master and skills to build. Working holidays and weekends, not because it was necessary, but because work was my favorite way to ignore the realities of life.

It always has been.

Even as a child, playing teacher or grocery store clerk, I knew how to assume the posture of hardworking adult as a distraction from the pain of being human.

It's not completely invalidated by society either. The world tells us to work hard, to lose sleep, and to succeed at all costs. Much of which is about patting ourselves on the back for the act of doing without a clear understanding of where we are going.

I think that's what makes work such a convenient distraction, because few people will argue with you when you say you have to work. Friends won't feel bad that you turned down their invitation, spouses know you're working hard for the family, and even you can start to believe that work really is that all-consuming. It's the perfect illusion.

With work as such a convenient distraction—the reminder that we are breathing in pain at every pause can be put off for another day—

And put off.

And put off.

And put off.

Until something breaks. A family member gets sick of it and makes an ultimatum. We come to grips with the fact that we're exhausting ourselves, or we look in the mirror one day and don't even know who we are anymore.

In that breaking point, we are invited into a new pattern. A new pace. A new way of being. But we often try to treat the behavior without looking at the cause of the problem. We try to work less.

But it itches.

It's uncomfortable, and we feel like our skin is made of ants that just want to do something already. Every cell in our body moving rapidly even though we are sitting still.

For me, when that happens, I usually give up. I convince myself that I'm someone who needs to be busy in order to be happy, and I start to make up more work to do. Selling it more convincingly this time so that no one will question my intentions.

But when we look underneath this need for progress, we can find the truth beneath the truth. "I like to work" starts to look a lot more like, "I'm scared of being lazy."

"I'm afraid that I'll let my family down," "It's my job to capitalize on the sacrifices my parents made," or even simply, "I'm unhappy."

And from there, we can start to heal.

And just like a wound that is starting to scab over, it may itch a bit for a while, but eventually the body regenerates, the scab goes away, and we forget that the itch was even there at all.

The trophy.

Have you ever felt like you were the trophy that your parents fought hard to earn?

A shiny, gold figure that they pull out to show their friends?

Your achievements the payment for the sacrifices they made.

And like the Indian in the cupboard—
Do you come alive when the spotlights go out?

When there is no need to perform, do your shoulders get to rest and
your essence come forward?

Where would you run to if no one was watching, and what would your
heart bring to life?

If the truth of who you are in the darkness were driving, how then
would you build your life?

Thrift stores.

I don't like shopping in thrift stores.

It's for the same reason I trained myself not to speak with a southern accent, or why I don't buy cereal in a bag no matter how broke I may be. It's my proof that I am not a product of my childhood.

This is obviously flawed logic, because I am, by the very laws of nature, a direct product of my childhood. That is the only thing that any of us can be.

But—

I don't shop at thrift stores, and I change the wash immediately after the washer finishes, because I never want the lingering smell of poverty on my clothes.

In my mind, it doesn't matter how much vanilla body wash I scrub into my skin, I will always smell like a moldy trailer and kerosene heat.

I don't think we always realize the severing we do in ourselves. One line drawn between me and my relationship to my father, one line drawn in attempts not to re-create the patterns of my mother, one line drawn at my sexual abuse, one line drawn from religious trauma, one line drawn at words said that I'd rather not hold on to, one line drawn at divorce, and so on. The more lines drawn, the less whole I feel. Like I've taken this perfectly good human and just erased all of the bits that make me uncomfortable until all that is left is a talking head that has learned to say the right things in order to get the job done.

It hurts so much to see what I've moved through. It hurts to remember the pain but also to remember my forgetting. As if that little girl who built me into the woman I am never really existed.

A job well done.

This is for the part of you that feels
As though your worth can be found in a blue ribbon—
A "job well done."
To the part that doesn't care which ladder you climb as long as you
    never stop climbing—even when the blisters start.
This is for the part of you that just needs a little tending to—even when
    there is work to be done.

Where do you go when the can-do attitude is too heavy to carry, and
you just want to lay down the act? Where do you breathe when the
air is made of money, and no matter how much you take in it's not
enough?

Where do you rest when the ladder keeps on climbing and the blisters
keep on forming and you're tired, but you fear stepping off?

And when did you last sing back into your heart?
Is it walking with you on this journey, or can you barely hear its beating
rhythm in the dark?

CONCLUSION

To the part in all of us that confuses accolades for love.

Not to brag, but when I was in the second grade, I cheered for the fifth and
sixth grade cheerleading team. It felt like a big deal at the time, and I spent
every afternoon practicing until I was forced to go to sleep. I valued the
feedback of my coach so much that I would come up with all of these extra
things to do in order for her to tell me I'd done a good job.

One week, I pulled her aside after practice to show her a dance that I'd
choreographed. I hoped she would see me as special and hardworking and
anything else that would fill the achievement-shaped hole in my heart.

To my initial delight, she loved the dance and asked me to teach it to the rest of the team at our next practice. Then the weirdest thing happened—that feeling of satisfaction lasted for barely an instant. No pride. No sense of fulfillment. No completion to this never-ending striving for approval.

I felt nothing, because the thing I've never told anyone until this moment is that I didn't make up that dance. I copied it step-by-step from an episode of *Full House*. Stephanie Tanner had a jazz recital, and I thought the dance was really cool, so I learned every step and taught it as my own.

And because of that, it felt empty. Every praise felt like someone was reminding me that it wasn't mine to hold. Even when I was able to convince myself that I'd really contributed to it somehow—it was like the compliments flew past me and onto whomever really deserved them.

This striving without fully being able to reap the reward keeps you hustling until you don't know when you're performing and when you're really dancing for the joy of it.

Into adulthood, this behavior can look like passing off ideas as your own, like I did with the dance. But it can also look like choosing to live a life based on what you think you're supposed to want and not what you actually want to do. It can look like going into debt for the things you think offer you status.

People compliment your expensive car, but you feel like a fraud because you're drowning in debt. People admire your impressive job, but you end every night unhappy and exhausted.

Strangers compliment your perfect family, but you feel alone.

The compliments evaporating as quickly as they're spoken.

When we put our worth in what we obtain, whether status, praise, or belongings, we are only ever able to see the value in what we own. This leaves us wondering if we're actually valuable ourselves.

If I'd learned that choreography for the joy of it and shared it as such, I would have been able to share my joy with my teammates instead of steeping in shame.

Similarly, if we build our lives out of the things that fulfill us—it doesn't matter how simple they are—our ordinary days become the most valuable thing we could ever possess.

CHAPTER FOUR

*

*To the part of you that fears
being average.*

INTRODUCTION TO TYPE FOUR

The Enneagram type four is commonly referred to as "the individualist" or "romantic." They are emotionally honest, comfortable with longing, and looking for their identity. This chapter is dedicated to the part in all of us that feels we must be understood in our wholeness in order to be loved. The part that fears they will never be known for who they truly are and seeks to find their significance from titles instead of being. In this chapter, we will address complex elements related to the Enneagram type four structure, such as:

1. Fearing the mundane

Type fours carry an undercurrent of pressure to find and express their significance—a sensation that they should be somehow set apart and special. The trouble is they are often comfortable with the space of failure, the romanticization of a starving artist or a secret genius. The area that they struggle with is the average middle on the way to being significant. The day-to-day discipline that it takes to make their way from unknown to known. The fear of getting stuck in average permeates so much that they may avoid it at all costs. The trouble is that anything significant we do must be made up of a bunch of average day-to-day tasks. The type fours who have inspired me with their growth have found a deep romanticization of average. The art of washing the dishes, the beauty in a beautiful spreadsheet, the magic of showing up every day to write. Through embracing the beauty in average, the type fours are able to shift from finding their significance and toward creating significance in how they live their life.

2. Being misunderstood

In all of us there is a longing to be known for the depths of who we are, none more so than our type fours. This focus of attention can be so all-consuming that being missed in even the simplest ways can make them feel as though they aren't known at all. The nuance to how they experience themselves being missed gives them the impression that they are completely misunderstood. The pain in this is that being completely known in the intricacies of how they see themselves is nearly impossible. Everyone will always let them down. The work is to learn to recognize love and knowing in the ways that they're being shown, even if they aren't exactly how you imagined them to be.

3. Digging into pain

There's a beautiful element of the type four structure that requires emotional authenticity. It seeks to feel all emotions to the maximum—both sadness and joy. Yet, sadness and longing can be something of a comfort zone, a place to go when the world feels shallow and wanting. I've heard type fours refer to this sadness as being much like a cozy blanket they can wrap around themselves to escape from the world. This can lead them to having a negativity bias—seeing only what is missing. It can lead to digging intentionally into negative emotions to keep the emotional hits coming. This is fine when it's the healthy aspect of allowing themselves to feel their feelings and self-validate. However, it can keep them stuck in states of anger, sadness, and shame when these emotions aren't allowed a natural release.

4. Preferring fantasy over reality

A rich fantasy life is one way that type fours find significance while avoiding the average. They create their success in their mind and avoid taking action in real life. They may fantasize about a relationship that has no issues while avoiding working on the relationship that they are in. They may think that something or someone will come in and rescue them, making it easier to be human, and they can take action when that happens versus making the reality that they crave for themselves. There's an importance in separating fantasy from reality. Owning that everyone and everything will disappoint you, that is real, and it is still very good. When things are real, they are flawed, and that does not make them less meaningful or right.

5. Seeking their wholeness outside of themselves

One of the core components of the type four structure is a sensation that they are missing something they need— others have this thing, and they are somehow missing it. The shape of this hole can change from a partnership to a college degree, to rich parents, or even just an amorphous concept of a thing that they feel but don't have words for. As they begin to explore the art of presence and grounding into reality, they will also shift their focus from seeking a sense of wholeness to embracing the wholeness that is already there. They will realize that they are good as they are, and any additional thing brought in is not a completion but an addition to who they are.

6. Comfort with longing

Naturally, if we are seeking something to fill us up, we are prone to fantasizing about a better reality and finding comfort in our sadness—we may find that longing is a place we often land. A comfort with wanting for more can propel beautiful action toward an idealistic lifestyle where every moment is treasured, and they don't settle for less than a meaningful existence. However, it can also discourage action and create a belief that there is so much to do that they will never get done, and they can just sit here in comfort—wanting—instead of out there in the cold—doing. It can look like longing for different relationships without ending old ones. It can look like longing for a new career without going through training. It can be a self-imposed limbo that keeps the type four comfortable but stagnant and unappreciative for all that they already possess both within themselves (i.e., character traits and talent—the talents of others always seeming more impressive) or relationships—the grass being greener in someone else's bed. The type four who harnesses their longing for fuel is able to keep it in its proper position. It's the drive that keeps them going rather than the lock that keeps them frozen.

Although they were written with the type four structure in mind, these essays and poems are an invitation to explore the part in each of us that feels we are not enough to be who we want to be. My hope is that they invite you to appreciate the present moment, become aware of all that you already are, and provide permission to feel loved even in love's inherent flaws.

"And" NOT "but."

I've often struggled as a parent with the balance of honoring my little one's emotions, while also teaching them the importance of gratitude. The complexity of holding both at once—the difficult and the beautiful. Learning how to respect and honor the full human experience without abandoning the understanding that there is so much good in the here and now.

Getting from the place of, "This is a terrible day and a terrible life," and letting it be, "This is a terrible moment, and it's overwhelming."

Allowing the emotions to be not only temporary but also specific to the situation at hand.

In my search for answers, I discovered the concept of "I'm lucky because . . ."

I stubbed my toe, I felt rejected at school, I'm tired of these shoes, and I'm lucky because I have a roof over my head.

All can exist at once.

"And" is an important word here, because so often I think we replace it with "but."

"I stubbed my toe, I felt rejected, I'm tired of these shoes, BUT I'm lucky because I have a roof over my head" isn't the same sentence or the same sentiment.

"But" implies we should feel something other than what we're feeling, that our gratitude is meant to replace the negative emotions we're experiencing.

"But" is treating gratitude like a pimple patch meant to cover and shrink our negative emotions instead of allowing them to come and go naturally.

For some, we can use gratitude as a method to fix our feelings, which doesn't solve our experiences; it only makes the flow of emotions more complicated. It forces them to sit in our bones, stagnant and writhing, until the patches just stop working, and they find a way to express themselves— through anger or lying or fear.

For others, we honor the emotions so much that gratitude tastes like salt on the tongue when what we're looking for is sugar. It feels like betraying the very nature of humanity and denying your truth by trying to fix or solve or look exclusively for the good.

The word "and" here allows for both to exist at once. No need to eliminate one or the other. A balance of salty and sweet. A dance with the joy and the pain.

YOU.

I can hear your heartbeat—a stampede of horses.
Wild and wonderful and deep.

And I know you feel the pulsing call to leave a YOU-shaped imprint on
    the world
Yet struggle to figure out what YOU is even shaped like.

And I know that when you think of everything you'd need—to be who
    you long to be—
It feels like your heart is wrapped around your body taking place of
    your skin.

Because surely—they have something you don't have or you would be
who they turned out to be.

And YOU feels like it's playing hide-and-seek taunting from the
bedroom closet—
Tucked safely out of sight—and no matter how many times you scream,
"Olly, olly oxen free"
You will never really find them.

And I hate to say that you have everything you need inside you already
Because it sounds so cliché.

But perhaps you're overlooking the glasses on top of your head while
complaining of not being able to see.

The middle place.

A pinprick pain can be so much more when we dig our fingers into it.
    A misheard word that reminds us of harm we once felt can be its own
form of trauma when we demand that it be heard.
    What starts as a flesh wound gets peeled at the edges until the entirety
of it is felt, honored, heard. It starts as a demand that our pain not be
ignored and ends as our wounds eating us alive.
    Now, I'm not saying that our feelings aren't worth being validated or
that we need to just think positively until the world gives us what we want.
Quite the contrary. However, there is a vast chasm of variety between toxic

positivity and swimming in our despair. One extreme asks us to ignore the realities of our suffering and think happy thoughts amid real abuse against ourselves and those more vulnerable. The other sinks us lower and lower into the belief that there is nothing here for us and nothing good can happen until we change the world.

Surely, we can find a middle place. The trouble, I think, is that the middle has often been complacent. We see it as average or as tolerant. If you stand in the middle, then what do you stand for? So we sink into one extreme or the other in an attempt to feel something—anything. Choosing to be a balloon whose weightlessness lifts us from being down-to-earth or choosing to be an anvil whose sturdiness can't be blown by the wind.

In my early twenties, I lived much like a balloon, floating from one entertaining moment to the next. Holding on to the belief that the world is working things out for me no matter what I do. Dancing my way through life, missing moments because I was too busy planning future adventures.

In my early thirties, I felt more like an anvil, sinking into the weight of all that has harmed me. Building up walls to keep out more pain. Insisting on every emotion being heard, validated, and accounted for.

Now, I just want to be a basketball. I expect for life to throw me against the wall, or I will lose a bit of air here and there, but in the midst of this, I trust that I'll always bounce back.

Words.

Those words you hold
Bundled in your arms like a baby in winter
Were never yours to carry.

The doubts you have
Flowing through your veins
Were never yours to inject into your system.

The stories you whisper to yourself
As you fall asleep about
Where you faltered and where you failed
Were never your standards to live up to.

There are so many words in a given day.
Thousands upon thousands of words.
Sometimes they burn into our brains
Like a brand meant for cattle.

Imprinting their symbol on our hearts
Becoming part of what defines us.

Sometimes positive words—
Pushing us to believe in who we are
Encouraging happy risks.

Sometimes dark words meant to cut,
Control, or manage our infinite potential.

We must talk back.
We must question their intent.
We must hold tightly to those that heal us
Placing them carefully over the ones that cut.

Significant.

For some, it is not enough to write a book. They must write a GREAT book. A book that is unlike any other book to ever be written. The pain here is that on the journey to writing a great book, you must first write lots and lots of very average things. What a shame it is that so many stop there—in the average. It's a shame to stop when you are in the phase of average, because average is so much better than terrible yet feels so far away from great. One can start to think that they may not be a writer of great books after all. That they must be somehow different from those who were born great. The secret, of course, is that no one is born great—or perhaps we are all born great. But talent, in and of itself, is a myth. We learn these things. We develop skills, we ask for help, and we grow. To pick up a pen and be immediately gifted—in my belief—is a tragedy. I wouldn't wish a lack of struggle on my worst enemy. It's in this process, the growth and the refining, that we are made.

There is no title that will give us the feeling that only struggle and development can provide. We hope to wear the title of artist or writer. That the title will show us that we are worthy, that we are, in fact, significant. Yet, a title without our battle with the mundane feels like wearing a shirt that doesn't fit right in the shoulders. A sense that it was made for someone else. When, in reality, it was meant for a version of ourselves that is to come—if we trudge through the average. The funny thing is that through the refining process, as we get comfortable with the journey to becoming great, the need for titles starts to slip away. We are no longer defined by being GREAT; instead, we fall in love with the part of us who keeps showing up, and instead of being concerned with writing the next great book, we are consumed with living the next great life.

Rough draft.

Sometimes, reading the work of a great writer makes you feel like you could write anything—like all of the words you've been looking for have finally fallen into place. Other times, reading a great writer makes you want to pluck your eyes out and cut a singular muscle in your hand that would make it hard for you to ever hold a pen again.

Perhaps it's the state of mind in which the words happened to find us. Maybe it depends on how much we've been writing lately. If we're feeling particularly prolific, then coming in contact with a brilliant writer is only a nudge in the direction we believe we're already going. But the weeks in which our pen seems to be on its last drip of ink—those writers are more a representation of who we will never be. The mental gymnastics that occur tell us that the writer must have sat down one afternoon, and it all just flowed out perfect like that. This discouraged part of us doesn't want to believe that there were rounds and rounds of revisions because then we'd have to trust that we, too, could make something great, and we are looking for evidence that we are uniquely not qualified for this dream.

Other bits of proof we easily find for this—our lack of writing recently, our distrust of the compliments we've received on our work so far, the breath that someone took once after reading our work before telling us they loved it, the one element of writing that happens to be hard for us even though we've never tried to improve and just expected the talent would show up one day AND IT HASN'T, and finally—perhaps the biggest one of all—that comment someone made about a poem we wrote in the third grade that we were really proud of but they just didn't get. We should have hung our hats up then.

Just as quickly as we plummeted—as if out of nowhere—we find our stride again. Usually because we've stepped away from our phones for a few days or we pushed through the discomfort, and we kept reading that great writer and something clicks and the words flow and hope returns, and we write and keep on writing until the next time someone's final product looks too shiny next to our rough draft.

Making diamonds.

Centuries we've watched
Read and listened to the
Completed works of those we admire—
The diamonds.

Final iterations that have tumbled
Through the hands of editors, critics,
And
Very
Honest
Friends.

Polished down
Fine-tuned
Changed from the
Rough rocks
That were their beginning.

And now we sit here
Our palms full
Of unpolished rocks
Letting them slowly fall
One
After
The
Other
Because they weren't born diamonds.

Notebooks.

I'm reminded today of the satisfaction we find in an empty notebook.

How so many of us purchase notebook after notebook only not to crack open its pages and make something out of it.

It's like the fact that the notebook is untouched is actually part of the appeal.

Perfect, clean, completely limitless in possibility without a flaw to be found.

The trouble is there are no great stories written on the pages of a notebook left untouched.

There is no magic dancing within the binding.

It is only the writing
The crossing-out
The lines started over
The coffee spilled on page 124
That tell us that it has lived.

It is in its attempts and its failings that we are able to truly fall in love with what the empty notebook even represents.

True love.

Why is it that most great love poems come from longing? A desire for someone you can't have, someone who is far away, or someone who is already gone?

It's as if the truest, most committed love isn't worthy of our admiration. But isn't that the good stuff? Isn't that what we should be celebrating? It's kind of revealing that we as a culture often overidentify with what we can't have. So much of our collective work has been releasing the idea that life has to be a constant struggle. That we have to hustle to earn our worth.

Like the goodness that is here and now isn't poetic enough? Like, is it love if I didn't have to eat myself alive to get it?

But I'll take the "long morning hugs, helping me carry my bags inside, taking the trash to the curb, asking me about my day, and knowing every single inch of my body, heart, and soul" kind of love.

I want poems about choosing to pause and listen instead of rushing through the conversation. Poems about putting your phone down and looking each other in the eyes because you want to make sure they know they matter. Poems about sharing your deepest shame and having the person across from you say, "That's what you're worried about? That's not that big of a deal." Poems about boundaries respected, childhood wounds being acknowledged, taking responsibility for our actions, and telling each other, "you're beautiful not because of what you've put on but because of the kind of person you are." This is the magic. This is the rest into love that we all deserve. Yet, it is so easily ignored for the longing.

Identity.

Be skeptical of your desire to seek an identity.

To apply a title to your existence.

Isn't it when we start to look for something to BE, we so often lose sight
of who we are?

The ache.

Perhaps you know the pain of feeling like you missed out on some very
important character trait.

Like your personality isn't what it should be in order to be loved for
who you are.

Perhaps you know the ache of feeling like no one truly gets you.

And sadly, that is OK with you because you're afraid if they did, they
wouldn't like you very much.

And maybe you know that in this pain, there is no room for convincing
you it's untrue.

Like some part of you feels like it could be an illusion but the loudest
part of you

Is too afraid of looking like a fool to take that chance.

Perhaps putting yourself out there truly and honestly feels like
Biting down hard on a piece of metal when you already have a
    toothache.
And though desperately you want to be valued for who you are,
You can't bear to take the risk of that not being good enough.

And maybe in those darker moments
When you are deciding to hide instead of shine
You can remember that there is nothing too human about you.
You are just as fallible as everyone else.

We are all here trying and failing and hoping to be loved for who
    we are.
And hiding your truth like a treasure in the closet
Is only prolonging your chance to meet those who know you're golden.

Dried flowers.

To me, dried flowers are one of life's most beautiful things. So uniquely
beautiful that they are incomparable to a fresh flower.

It is beautiful in its own right.

A flower that has lived a full life, and its petals tell the story of richness
and of depth.

But I wonder if the flower feels that way. Does it know that it only
grows separate in beauty?

It's not MORE beautiful than a fresh flower but it's also not less beautiful in anyway.

It's just beautiful—differently.

I wonder if the dried flowers feel as though they smell like rotting flesh—they are dying after all. Do they fear that makes them less desirable? Or perhaps they think that being dried is superior. That the fragility and abundance of fresh flowers makes them boring or even common.

Are they so focused on what they aren't that they fear they are less worthy than a flower just cut, or are they consumed with the sensation that they have a secret knowing of what it means to be sophisticated and timeless?

I wonder if they—like me at times—struggle to hold the tension of feeling like they aren't enough but also maybe that they're too much?

The other flowers chattering on about how they're dramatic while the dried ones just refuse to ignore the pain that is all around.

The petal clenching thirst of a life fully felt.

The darkened petals that seem to whisper, "I know the ache of asking if anyone would notice that I'm gone." The beauty of a flower that has looked at the potential of loss and stayed to tell the tale.

There is an unarguable magic in a dried flower that I think comes not from its superiority, but from its separateness. Sure, it is a bit dramatic to hang a floral corpse from a windowsill or a wall. But it tells a story of a life lived and lost. The suffering that it takes to make it to something new and beautiful and changed.

I see the same magic in the eyes of those who are sensitive to life's subtleties. The ones who've been told they're too much for wanting to stop discussing the weather and start discussing where you learned to store your heartache. And the deepening of beauty that happens when they no longer seek a place above or below. No longer questioning am I bad or am I better than—simply stepping to the side and making something rich out of their own experiences.

The art of feeling and sharing what they've seen.

This magic when valued turns the personal into something universal. Their stories of living and feeling and change become tiny road maps that help the rest of us to feel less alone being human. Allowing us the freedom to no longer question am I enough or am I too much, but instead to say—I am beautiful in my own right.

CONCLUSION

To the part in all of us that longs to be understood.

When I was about ten or so, I took a rowboat out on the lake behind my grandparents' house with my brother. We were fighting over who got to paddle, and he had been greedy with his turn.

Years later, I came home from college and walked into a room of people who'd watched this encounter on video. None of them able to hear the subtle taunting my brother had done but hearing only my insistence that he share—my screeching.

I felt hot shame rise into my face, and tears flew faster than I was prepared for.

It felt awful to be misunderstood in this way.

They couldn't see that I was trying in every area of my life to just be good.
I wanted for nothing else than to be good. Yet, here was a glaring reminder
that I could never be. To make it worse, I felt dramatic and ashamed of
being so sensitive about something that happened such a long time ago.
I can hear my mother's voice, "You've always been tenderhearted," as I
rushed from the room.

I think at the core of this moment was the fear that I just didn't feel known by
my family. That I'd been missed. And then to build on that concern—my tears
told a story of a sensitive little girl, but I didn't feel like a sensitive little girl—I
felt strong and offended. I wanted to be known. I wanted to be respected.

I wanted to be seen for the fullness and the complexity of that moment and
of my past.

That feeling is the emotional equivalent of buying one thing with a giraffe
on it, and then all of the sudden everyone thinks you're really into giraffes,
so they buy you giraffe-related things for the next ten years. Until one day
you have to tell them that you aren't that into giraffes, and they have no
idea where that came from because your house is covered in giraffe-related
things.

They picked up on one subtle piece of information—latched onto it, and
now that's the story of who you were and who you will always be. A
screeching little girl. A person obsessed with giraffes.

Like taking a beautiful origami swan and flattening it out to a simple sheet of paper because that is easier to understand.

I think for some of us, the pain of being misunderstood is so vivid and visceral that it feels like a rumbling in our chest. Yet, it seems as though so few people truly want to see and be seen. They try to name the unnamable—claiming our experiences as simple and clear. Their attempt to feel as though they already know us, preventing them from getting to know who we continue to become.

I think it's the respect for evolution that makes this process so difficult but also so meaningful. The feeling of being misunderstood occurring because we continue to grow and change, making it hard to pin us down. But if we find ourselves in dialogue with those who aren't open to new understandings, then it feels like explaining trigonometry to a five-year-old. It's a waste of our time.

And the guarded part of me wants to dismiss them as shallow or simple. But the tenderest part of me fears no one will ever truly know me, and because of that, I am alone.

As with most things, this is a case of both. Yes, I want more from these relationships, *and* I am not alone just because people don't see me the way I hope they will in that moment. I can be missed slightly and still seen mostly. I can be loved and not fully understood—especially in the nuance of what that means for me.

It can be imperfect but still be very good.

CHAPTER FIVE

*

To the part of you that fears depletion.

INTRODUCTION TO TYPE FIVE

The Enneagram type five is commonly referred to as "the observer" or "the investigator." They are logical, emotionally private, and seek to be informed. This chapter is dedicated to the part in all of us that withdraws when the world is too intense. The part that fears depletion and seeks to understand the world around them. In this chapter, we will address complex elements related to the Enneagram type five structure, such as:

1. Disconnection from their body

When you seek to understand the world intellectually, it can be easy to believe that the world can be experienced through your mind. It's common for the type five structure to live as though the body is what is present from the neck up. Forgetting to check in with how they feel, what sensations are happening in their body, and even what it feels like to be alive. They can get so consumed with their mental processing they may forget the power and information that is held in the body. When talking with type fives about the first thing they can do on their growth journey, I typically say to start an embodiment practice. That could be a yoga nidra meditation or even just a daily walk—anything to remind them that they have a body that's storing tons of information for them.

2. Compartmentalization

It can be helpful and orderly to keep things separate, whether that's emotions separate from decision-making or work friends separate from family friends. It keeps things organized and tempered. I think of the type five mind like a child's dinner plate—nothing can touch. This, of course, can be unsustainable as they create more and more necessary intimacy. People tend to want to feel integrated into your life, and this can be a bit of a struggle for some type fives. It may feel like their spaces are being invaded. Another reason this can happen is because masking is a way to hide in plain sight. Performing a personality that matches that of the group can let you blend in with the crowd and go more unnoticed. With several friend groups or people they're committed to, it can feel disorienting to blend them because the type five may show up differently with each of them.

3. Privacy

Type fives can often be mistaken as unemotional. However, they have emotions just like the rest of us. They just tend to limit their expression of them. They may keep their true feelings private as well as their information. In general, they are guarded about how much they share with others. I've had it described to me before as feeling as though someone is trying to take from you when they are seeking personal information. This is another way that our type fives may limit their opportunity for genuine connection with others. Hiding themselves behind the masks mentioned above or literally hiding themselves by keeping details about who they are and how they're feeling a secret.

4. Fear of depletion

Depletion of resources is a major area of concern for type fives. The fear that they will not have what they need to meet the demands placed on them is a constant juggling act of dosing out their energy, money, and time to different areas demanding their attention. This can lead to hoarding of resources as a preventive measure, making their needs really small as not to have to ask for anything from anyone. This is a skill that many of us need to learn—to balance our resources and give ourselves plenty of time to rest. However, when used to the extreme, it can prevent type fives from taking action on the things they're passionate about or showing up fully in their relationships. The art is in finding the spot where this skill is used at the right time and in the right place.

5. Retreating in relationships

If you fear depletion, prioritize your privacy, and like to keep your life compartmentalized, it makes sense that one of your major attributes will be retreating within relationships. Seeking time alone to think, to work on passion projects, to sit comfortably in silence. This is a natural response to fear of overstimulation. However, many times the type five doesn't communicate their intentions or an intended end time to their time alone. So the people in their life are left wondering if they've done something wrong or if the type five wants to be around them at all. This concern can often be solved with increased communication, which does require the type five to give up some sense of privacy and control. Which, if they are honest with themselves, is the least they can do to preserve their relationships.

6. Self-reliance

Somewhere along the way, type fives learned to fend for themselves. It could be because they had caregivers who were so overbearing that they learned to fend for themselves to keep them at arm's length, or for some, it could be their parents were absent or negligent, so they learned that they could only rely on themselves. Either way, they seek to keep a balance of how much they give and how much they receive. Living with the mentality of, "I take care of myself, and you take care of yourself, and we are good." This would work great except that we are communal beings who do rely on one another to get our needs met. Whether that's time or food or emotional support—we all at some point or another will need each other. Additionally, it makes life harder than it has to be. Managing day-to-day life alone is logistically just more work. Although many type fives will limit their needs in order to make it more possible to be self-reliant, they often miss out on many of life's pleasures in the process.

Although they were written with the type five structure in mind, these essays and poems are an invitation to explore the part in each of us that feels we must hide from the world. My hope is that they invite you to reach an empowered sense of right action, believe that you have more to give than you realize, and offer permission to ask for support.

Shell.

One morning I went outside to find a turtle waiting at our front door.

We live about half a mile from a lake that is full of red-eared sliders, and I imagine that's where he ventured over from.

The walk to the lake isn't an easy one, though—even for us. There's no sidewalk and there are lots of curves that the cars fly around blindly. I have become someone who prays every morning when my husband takes his run to the water's edge. I tell you that to say, if it feels that dangerous to us, then how on earth did this little turtle make its way to my doorstep without a scratch?

While my husband and son found a box to carry him back to his home, I was meant to keep an eye on him. While we stood there, I felt a longing to connect with this turtle. A desire to make eye contact and feel that even though we are different, we are also the same. That creeped the turtle out, and he went right into his shell.

I thought how nice it must be to have a place to go when the world is too much. When it feels like people are crowding in around you, and you have nothing left to give. A place that is only there for you and your thoughts. And I suppose that may be how this turtle made its way here so safely. Knowing when to stop and take breaks, knowing when to go inside for respite, and who to let in and who to keep at arm's length.

And I thought about you, how you retreat when the world is too loud. How it is likely what's helped you get to where you are safely. Your shell is your privacy—a barrier that has allowed you to survive up to this point, and I am so grateful for it (as I imagine you are too).

And, as I'm sure you are aware, the turtle must exit its shell eventually. It took steps to find its way to my doorstep. It peeks out to eat, swim, bask, and make love. That's the beautiful thing about gifts. When we use them intentionally, they can be the very thing that keep us going. Yet, when used at the wrong time or in the wrong place or used just a bit too often, they can be the thing that keep us from experiencing love, safety, and nourishment.

It's not a shame to have a shell. In fact, many of us could learn to build one. It's just about knowing when to enter and when to exit and who to share it with along the way.

Feelings and facts.

This morning, my husband noted a small change in my facial expression, and to my complete and utter surprise, he asked me what was wrong.

I didn't know I'd had a feeling.

All I know is that sometimes the world feels too much for my skin.

Each sound a vibration taking a little bit away from what I thought I had to give.

And the jury in my mind is deciding which things I'm allowed to feel that day. How much energy to take from my body to my head, or if it could all just be solved and not felt.

The jury prefers reason and logic and facts. Intense emotions feel unpredictable and strange. My jury often says, "We don't have time for that," or "If you wait long enough, this will all go away."

So I float up safely and lie in the crevice of my mind, leaving my body to fend for itself.

A hollow tree walking and talking with my brain holding the levers, like an old Power Rangers movie.

But once—as my jury deliberated how much I was allowed to feel—my love asked me where it was happening in my body, and there I was.

Whole and honest and raw. The truth of what was happening sitting tight in my chest, fully ready to talk as soon as I would bear witness.

And this also works for joy. An attempt at silencing all that my body wants to share—a rejection of intensity, both of the bad and of the good.

So that a wonderful day gets digested intellectually as a day like any other and my smile gets softened so that I'm not too obviously giddy, and I limit the freedom in my expression so that I don't get carried away.

But every once in a while, the jury takes a breather, and I forget to play the judge, and a large dose of pleasure seeps in, and I am like a child laughing in the church pews. A joy bellowing from deep in my soul that is only heightened for fear of getting caught off guard.

Coffee on social media.

On the weeks when I'm offline
My morning coffee is a symphony.
A tiny, precious moment that feels miraculous every time.
The way coffee mixes with milk to create a completely new flavor.
The way milk sweetens up when you heat it just right.
The way no matter how many years I drink this day after day it's still
       something I wake up looking forward to like it's the first time.
My attention is here on this moment with this experience, and it is bliss.

On weeks when I am plugged in

My morning coffee is a routine.

A mindless pattern that I step into without really noticing.

I feel like the conversation in my mind is being interrupted by real-life people wanting to share with me.

My thoughts are a mixture of worries, to-do lists, and embarrassing memories of things I wish I hadn't said.

I try to enjoy the moment, to slow down and really pay attention, but it's like my mind is the rope in a game of distraction tug-of-war.

Your mind is a container store.

Your mind is a container store.

Each consideration tucked away into a tidy, little box.

Work in a box on the shelf high on aisle three.

Friends from childhood on the shelf below the ones you met in adulthood.

Each area relegated to its own zone—tightly sealed and kept apart.

And then there is love.

Like a scene from an alien movie, its tentacles are knocking at the seal on its box demanding access to every other compartment.

Its sticky arm reaching—threatening to disrupt the perfect equilibrium that you've maintained for so long.

The effort it takes to keep shoving love back into its container. Holding the lid as it tries to escape makes you question if it's worth the effort.

But love keeps knocking, asking the question—what do you do when there are things that can't be organized with your mind but can only be felt with your heart?

Grief out loud.

When I'm sad, I feel like a feral cat. I want to hide under the car and hiss at anyone who gets close. It's embarrassing to be seen in my weakness. Like I'm giving a part of myself away to them. Like they can drink my tears and take my power.

So I hide it away and give it to private moments and write about it and share it once the pain has left me stronger. The one in control of my story. But grief came in and ripped me open. As I write to you, I'm sitting on a bench in a park in Savannah, Georgia, smiling at strangers in between shaking sobs. It's ninety degrees out and so humid that I can chew the air. I have a bright-yellow bow in my hair and sorrow in my bone marrow. I know how to crinkle my eyes so that people think I'm happy, but my hands are shaking so much that I can't really grip my pen.

Why this pain? Why is this the one that cracked me open and keeps the salt water pouring out? Why not my grandfather who was more of a dad to me, anyway?

Perhaps it has to do with watching my husband care for our son. Seeing how he tenderly engages with his feelings, lovingly puts him to bed, and keeps improving himself as he seeks to love his son better.

I didn't have this close-up picture of a father before I met him. I didn't know what people had. I didn't know what I'd been missing. I've put those pieces together over the years and even processed it a bit with my husband and my therapist. But I guess I hadn't really grieved it.

I'm also trying to feel things these days. The desire to close off and rationalize it is hindered with the awareness of the havoc it can wreak on your body and your mind. Knowing that my one functioning kidney is already experiencing a degree of distress while my lungs struggle to breathe is enough for me to know that I can't keep ignoring my pain. At some point, you have to slow down and just feel things. Fear, sadness, anger, terror, memories—all of it.

That's where I am, and while it's awkward and makes me feel uncomfortable, and like a bit of a burden or a charity case, I am also so very happy to feel alive. I am happy to know that this, too, is just part of being human. It's part of living a life wide open, digging my fingers into the damp soil of sorrow, and making art out of dirt.

Amateur.

I find delight in embracing the role of amateur—this space between beginner and expert.

I revel in this so much that once someone left a review on a survey of mine saying that it's what they most disliked about my approach. That I won't go all in and claim my expertise.

It's just that "amateur" implies I have more to learn, and I never want to be someone who thinks they've got it figured out. I don't want to age like a fossil who hardens as the years go by. Instead, I want to age like a tree who adds rings to their knowledge year by year by year.

Putting yourself out there.

Putting yourself out there can feel like
Laying out to tan when you have a sunburn.

Eyes searing into your already blistered skin.

Sometimes, I open up my messages and wince
At the fear of a painful hand across my back.
But often it's just aloe.
Lovely humans connecting with me in our odd futuristic way.

I'm convinced we aren't evolutionarily ready for this.

The constant feedback on everything we do.

Surely that is more than our systems are built to handle.

Sometimes I imagine that everyone here is in a room with me

Hundreds of thousands of people all yelling, "I like this."

"That's not quite right."

"You should try essential oils!"

"Where did you get that lamp?"

It would all be too much.

Yet, we show up here every day

As if the internet is not real life and expect ourselves to operate

As though it doesn't impact us.

But how is that fair to our souls and our skin?

When?

How many books will you read before you write one of your own?

How many podcasts will you binge before you purchase a microphone?

And how many times will you stand on the precipice of starting only to
tell yourself there is one more thing to know?

A partner's perspective.

I wish I could pour love into the space between your heart and your walls. A thick molasses message that you are never too much to be seen. But I know that love feels like hooks in the cheek when it comes with expectation—so I knock, and I wait. Tell me, how do you tell the difference between boundaries and isolation?

When has it gone on too long?

And where do you put your feelings when you have them? Mine don't fit so easily in a box.

And how do I know that I'm wanted when you're ready if you don't tell me you're leaving before you're gone?

Love versus sacrifice.

This morning, I sat and watched the roofers fix the house next door. Heating and laying down tar one square at a time. I was reminded of rebuilding homes in New Orleans the year after Katrina.

I've experienced nothing like the overwhelming sight of an entire wall of a naked home that I was meant to dress one nail and one strip of vinyl at a time.

Even now as I write to you, I can remember the sense of hopelessness. The fear that it would take all day. That I would break in the process of pushing past my perceived limits. Feeling as though it was too much. Too big of a task.

I learned to focus on just the next nail and not to look at all that was ahead of me. One more nail, one more piece of vinyl, and remembering why we were there. The person who would benefit from our efforts and why the work we were doing was hard, but it was not an exhaustion for nothing. It was an exhaustion for something. For someone.

Each nail another step toward getting someone back in their home.

One more nail.

One more strip of vinyl.

One step closer to a home.

When I forgot why we were doing this and focused instead on the hot Louisiana sun beating down on my ginger skin, my lack of sleep, or the aching in my back from squatting at the same level for nail after nail after nail, I would want to flee. To free myself from the obligation of doing too much.

After all, people need sleep—we need time alone to rest, and my skin would blister in the sun. My mind racing with reasons why this was too much to ask of myself. Too much to give.

Then I would remember the people. The humans whose home I was putting back together one nail at a time. The memories they'd lost. The fear they must hold and the loss that turned my stomach when I thought of it.

And I spoke their names and words of love one nail at a time.

Sharon.

Marcus.

Gigi.

Dan.

Each name a reminder that I can do more than I think I can.

Through this, I have learned that it is much easier to love than to over-sacrifice. When I focus on how much I am giving and what is being taken from me, I wither at the thought of giving more.

Yet, the same action done in love breathes life into my bones and my capacity grows tenfold.

On support.

Is it cozy, the place you go to in your mind?
And is it lined with rich leather books and smelling gently of
    sandalwood like I always imagined?
Have you found a way to solve your need to be supported?
Is it true that if you want for nothing, then no one can intrude upon
    your innermost thoughts?
Tell me—when you climb out of your head one limb at a time stretching
    to meet the world, is it uncomfortable to remember you have a
    body?
I wonder—how small can you make your needs before we don't realize
    you are there?
And who taught you that it was better to get by on little rather than
    relying on someone else?

Do you have the phrase "It's better to be seen and not heard" playing on
    repeat?
Because I worry that you're carrying far more than you have to do
    alone.

And when your heart breaks—like glass in a million pieces—
Do you call someone, or do you climb one limb after the other back to
the library in your mind?

CONCLUSION

To the part in all of us that learned to only rely on ourselves.

One early evening when I was around seven years old, I sat in the tall grass across the street from my home. The lights on the inside of the trailer illuminating everything I was hiding from and the crickets in surround sound unable to drown out the yelling from inside.

I crouched behind the grass hiding as my brother fought the battle inside. I was jealous of the freedom he had to stand like wrought iron in the middle of the storm. To claim his voice even when everything seemed to say there wasn't time for that.

I imagined my own bravery. Standing with my chest toward the grown-ups puffed and proud. A voice that came from my gut and made them tremble with its earnestness. But I always seemed to keep my words to myself for fear of it coming out more like a whimper.

So I sat among the grass while my brother fought our battles for us, and I drew up maps of all the places I would go. Sometimes, I packed bags, walked a mile up the road, and sat under the bridge that went over the creek, where I'd catch crawdads on happy days. Other times, I just played in our secret spot in the woods listening to the sound of the water while making childish pottery out of the red clay mud.

This particular day, I stayed there hidden among the bushes watching my life from the outside, and I escaped in my mind. I created a world where there was no need for fighting or for running. A world where problems could be solved with logic, and people were so rational that intense emotions didn't have to exist.

When the sun set behind the hilltops, I made my way inside, prepared to be chastised, or even fretted over, but the chaos had subsided, and no one seemed to know that I had gone. I realized then that I had run away a long time ago, sinking further and further into my own world as my presence became smaller and my imagination grew larger.

If I'm honest, as a child, I think I liked it that way: no one making a big fuss over me; no intensity over me at all. I felt invisible, and that privacy made me feel strong.

However, with some decades of seeking love later—I grieve for that version of myself. The little girl that needed to be searched for. The one who should have been more important than whatever fight was going on. I realize now that the pain of wanting to be seen was there, even if it came out like a stifled whimper.

CHAPTER SIX

*

*To the part of you that fears
letting others down.*

INTRODUCTION TO TYPE SIX

The Enneagram type six is commonly referred to as "the loyalist" or "the loyal skeptic." They value safety and community and prefer to be prepared. This chapter is dedicated to the part in all of us that fears being left without support. The part that tests authority and seeks to guarantee a positive outcome. In this chapter, we will address complex elements related to the Enneagram type six structure, such as:

1. Loyalty

Support is a high need for those with the type six structure. They create alliances and develop relationships, ensuring they are not without support or guidance. With this comes a dedication to relationships and a desire to stay connected. This can lead them to remain loyal to relationships, jobs, or personal choices even when they question if that's what is best for them. The releasing of this allows for the type six to choose what is best for themselves, even if it may let someone else down, thus recognizing that their disappointment is temporary, but this is their one precious life.

2. Skepticism

If you are particularly loyal to the people in your life, it makes sense that you may be a bit particular about the people, ideas, and activities that get into your life. Many type sixes prefer to keep people at arm's length until they are certain that they can be trusted. With practice and mindfulness, the type six can learn to use this skill when necessary but to allow room for more trust when little is at stake.

3. Questioning

The type six structure is a cautious one that seeks certainty. At times, those with the type six structures may convince themselves that they do not know what is best. They may seek lots of outside counsel when making decisions. They may give their authority away to others. They may stay in indecision as they attempt not to make the wrong choice. I had a type six tell me once that they assume their friends and family know what's best for them even when it's on a topic that the type six was more qualified to address. This consistent questioning can lead to indecision, playing devil's advocate, disconnection with self, and stalling progress. As type sixes begin to build self-trust, they are more able to listen to their adept intuition and separate that from their fear.

4. Fear of change

When value is placed on certainty, support, and safety, it prioritizes what is known. What can be predicted and accounted for. It can make big or even small changes feel like it's too large of a risk. They may prefer to stick to the familiar as a way to guarantee a positive outcome. This ultimately limits their access to new experiences that could deeply enrich their life. Allowing themselves to take small risks opens them up to taking larger risks, which can be very rewarding in the long-term goal of living a fulfilled life.

5. Being prepared

"Fear" is the word most associated with the structure of type six. Whether this is an overt fear or a covert fear depends on the individual. However, every type six has some relationship to fear. A pattern of worst-case-scenario thinking. However, it doesn't always feel this clear to the type six individuals. I have found it helpful to rephrase this as "preparation." A desire to be prepared—to guarantee a positive outcome. At the end of the day, the type six structure is seeking a guarantee of some kind. A certainty in the right beliefs, the right career, the right relationships. They seek that certainty through loyalty, testing, resisting change, and being prepared.

6. Relationship to authority

Perhaps the most complex element of the type six is their relationship to authority. On one hand, they seek to find an ultimate authority that they can rely on for support. On the other hand, they're afraid of authority having too much control. They test authority to ensure that they can be trusted, and that trust isn't given easily. At the same time, they can be very loyal to authority once the trust is earned. My favorite quote from a type six on this topic was, "I don't want to be the boss, but I want to hire the boss." They want someone else to guide and give expectations that they can follow, but they want to make sure that that person is someone they respect and admire.

Although they were written with the type six structure in mind, these essays and poems are an invitation to explore the part in each of us that is seeking a sense of certainty. My hope is that they invite you to an opening to adventure, a place of inner peace, and permission to let people down as you fight for yourself.

Birdhouse.

There's an old birdhouse in our backyard that I am oddly attached to. My husband and our neighbor have both expressed interest in replacing it with a nice, new one, but I refuse.

There is something beautiful to me in its weathered roof, chipping paint, and the way it leans far to the left like an old tree who's tired of standing tall.

I realize that a new birdhouse would be beautiful in its own way, and it would probably do a better job at being an actual birdhouse. But I can't imagine a life looking out the window across a yard full of leaves and flowers and snow without the one that I know.

This birdhouse watched me tour the home in fear that we wouldn't have anywhere else to go.

It watched us move in on that first summer without enough furniture to fill the rooms.

It watched during that season I tried to get into jump rope and the hours of writing my husband has done at the dining room window.

It watched as my son finally started playing outside by himself and my first attempt at a garden grown in pots: first by the driveway and the next year on the patio—both starting strong and ending as food for the deer.

It watched us go from timid and transient to making this space our home.

It is a part of our story. A vessel that holds our memories in its Swiss cheese walls, and I love it.

I am reminded of a friendship I'd held on to much the same.

Every unkind word floating off me like it didn't leave a stain.

Each night of being told that my experience could be solved, and she had the answers.

The night being left drunk and alone in a bar with a strange man walking home at midnight in a snowstorm, because she was meant to be my ride.

All the cracks and the chips were beautiful because she'd borne witness to my life for a time.

It was a cold fall day on a lake in Canada that I had a conversation with someone I'd known for a moment and felt more seen and accepted than I had with this friend of several years. They listened and were present, and I saw what it would be like to have a friendship with proper support.

And I suppose it will be the same when my husband replaces this birdhouse and sturdies up its foundation.

A beautiful reminder that what we tolerate will remain until we change what we withstand.

Dogwoods.

I can tell if it's a good day by the way I think about the dogwood trees.

Are they a miracle that occurs for ten days once a year, and I'm so lucky to get to witness them?

Or is it a shame that they'll be gone soon, and I'm a failure for not making the most of them while they're here?

The humming.

My husband and I often talk about how the world sounds different on the day that the trash gets taken out.

We wake up to the slow, steady rumble of trucks being dispersed across the city. A low-level humming hours before they even arrive at our driveway. The streets carrying the song, "Have you forgotten something this morning?"

The foundation-shaking rumble mirrors the one at home in my chest as I've had to wrestle with my family and my values. Do I stand for what I believe in, or do I make peace with the ones I love?

The contradicting loyalties an earthquake of confused priorities.

My mind harmonizing with the streets, "Have you forgotten where you come from? Don't forget who you've become!"

On presence.

How many steps ahead is your mind from your body? Is it running to
    the corner to make sure there's nothing around the bend?
And how far away are the concerns that you carry?
Is it making sure to pack sunscreen, or is it just a little extra in the
    savings before real life can begin?

And how hard do you work to be the one they can trust?
While not being certain of who you can truly rely on?

And are you tired from all the scanning that tells you there is something
    to fear?

Or are you so comfortable in preparing that it doesn't even feel like
    anxiety anymore?

When is the last time you took a really good breath?
Or noticed the sun as it predictably rises and sets?

And can you believe me when I say that right here,
In this moment,
You are safe?

A familiar risk.

Our toilet broke last night, and that set off a series of events that have me
sitting in the McDonald's across from my house writing to you.

I've never stepped inside this McDonald's before and have definitely
never thought of it as a lovely place to write, but here we are, and I'm
finding it comforting to watch the people who seem to come here every day.

A man offered me his paper after he finished reading it, and then we
talked for a while. He said his wife calls him the social director. He comes
here every morning ever since he retired. He takes the newspaper from his
driveway and picks up the *Wall Street Journal* from the post office on his walk
over, and he reads and makes calls before the dining room fills up. He said
there's a table of people who sit at the corner by the window that he calls
the Liars' Club—which is conveniently the title of a memoir I recently read.

I thought of all the times I've been a regular somewhere and how at home that's made me feel. The same experience time and time again. Comfortable small talk with people who've become not quite friends but neighbors.

There's a table of older friends that started as coffee for two, and one by one, someone walks in and joins them. Their laughs bouncing off the ceiling, making me envy their age. I've drawn the unfair conclusion that they do this every day or at least once a week. They all knew to show up somehow and seem not to need much time joining into the running conversation.

Being a regular feels like the adult version of my kid watching the same show over and over again. It's comforting. Familiar. Predictable.

No monsters are jumping out of a closet—at least none that you aren't prepared for.

There is safety in repetition. A seeming guarantee of a good experience. A lessened likelihood of loss.

Yet, in these regularities, there is always a beginning and an end.

This now-familiar experience was once something we did for the first time. A risk that we took. A restaurant we could have hated, a job we could have failed, a movie or a person we didn't know we'd love.

And at the same time—

Restaurants close, we get fired or we retire, every relationship eventually comes to some form of an end.

I watch the man at the table across from me—back-to-back with the group of people whose laughter filled the room—and I wonder if he started coming here alone or if he is simply the last one still showing up.

His presence reminds me that the things that become our comforts were once a risk we took that will eventually be a source of loss. But it doesn't make them less meaningful in the in-between. It is worth the risk, and it is worth the inevitable loss to have loved something for a time.

On self-trust.

Be cautious of anyone who tells you who you are.
The ones who want you to trust their understanding of
You over how you know yourself.

They have not dipped their toes into the innermost parts of your being.
They have not been in your head as you convinced yourself to wake up
    in the morning
And they are not privy to the parts of you that you know how to hide
    so well.

Instead, ask yourself—what do they have to gain from me trusting them
    over myself?
And set yourself free.

Leaves of summer.

I've been dreading the end of summer, wanting to hold on to the last few weeks of bare shoulders and sun-kissed skin. As others are getting excited for the switching of seasons, I can't help but smell the frigid winds of winter in the changing of the leaves.

This morning, I sat and watched the squirrels jump from tree limb to tree limb, acorns bared between their teeth. They, too, are preparing for winter.

So, this morning, as I considered the changing of the seasons, I invited myself to notice. The trees are still fully stocked with leaves—not empty and dwindling as I'd imagined. The moss is still neon green peeking out from the cracks in the sidewalk. I could still breathe in the morning air without a sharpness in my lungs.

For days, as the leaves danced in the wind making their way from sky to earth, I've felt dread. A sense that all the good is coming to an end. Yet, the tree closest to our window is turning orange around the edges, and when I really look at it—it's so beautiful I could cry.

Each leaf a different shade from green to brown to orange. A miracle of nature that I could easily ignore for fear of the coming storms.

That's just it, isn't it? As we seek to hold on to the good that was, we become scared of what's to come, which causes us to miss all that is already here.

Leaves of fall.

Every year when fall arrives
On a cozy rainy day
My husband will gaze out the window and say,
"All of this rain will make the leaves fall too quickly."

I laugh because it's predictable, but I understand because there is
    something unsettling about happiness.
All of the sudden there is so much to lose.

Attraction becomes potential heartbreak.
A new home is a possible eviction notice.
Raised standard of living becomes a longer way to fall from the top.
Marriage is the daily act of not getting a divorce.

I have found that when I see my joys as potential pains, I become a back
    seat driver to my life.
An outside observer who is no longer participating but has a lot of
    things to say.

I try to control the emotions of those I'm in relation to out of fear that
    they will leave.
I budget with a vengeance as to never have to worry about paying
    the rent.
I limit my access to small joys for fear of being frivolous.
I grasp too tightly to my marriage for fear of us drifting apart.

But, perhaps with these things, it is just like the leaves—our job is not to
　　prevent the loss or to control the possible outcome.
Our job is to be here.
To see them for the good that they are in the moment.
To allow them to be beautiful even in their impermanence.

On playing devil's advocate inside your own mind.

I watched a video once of a gorilla being tranquillized.
　　Each giant limb falling in slow motion.
　　It was unsettling how something so powerful can be taken down by
something as small as a needle.
　　I wondered if its mind was still racing as its body lay dormant, like mine
does when I am stuck in indecision.
　　The tranquillizing feeling of playing a round of mental ping-pong,
where the only player is myself.
　　Rushing toward certainty only to be bombarded with a bucket full of
perspectives bouncing in every direction.
　　A cascade of
　　Ifs
　　Ands
　　Buts
　　And certainty is like a mirage in the desert. Everything in me wants to
drink—to quench my thirsting mind—but it's gone as quickly as it appears.

And when someone offers me their canteen like they know it's full and safe—it seems to vibrate with alarm bells ringing.

How do you trust something that claims to have all the answers when the questions are still bouncing violently in your mind?

Each turn of devil's advocate a step forward on the path to my certainty oasis but every other one a step back in pursuit of thinking things through.

Perhaps a place of stillness could be built in the middle place where ideas and thoughts cross over.

A witness stand to notice as the game keeps going on.

Confusion and clarity.

I heard someone say recently
That confusion preempts clarity.
And I'm not sure why, but I know it's true.

The moments where I feel stuck in indecision,
Although intolerable at the time, eventually fade
And like a painting in your church basement, the
clouds part and the sun shines down and
The path is clear.

In the moment, though, it's like my arms are reaching across the chasm
Grasping for a new life
While my heels dig deep into the cliffs that they're familiar with.

And even though my muscles are shaking, I can't seem to decide if I
should push my feet forward or bring my hands back, so
There we stay stuck and in pain.

Clinging desperately to the old
While begging for the new.

CONCLUSION
To the part in all of us that has a complicated relationship with authority.

When I was in the eighth grade, my stepfather was at the peak of his
addiction, my friends at school had turned into bullies, and my teacher was
straight out of a coming-of-age film where the protagonist could never do
anything right. I was being put in suspension for responding to the bullies,
and my grades were falling as I managed the stress of home and social life.
I would go home every day crying to my mom about school while she was
navigating her own crisis with her marriage. It felt as though there was
nowhere safe to go. My mom suggested I move in with my grandparents and
try school in Florida.

During my childhood, I often found respite in the home of my maternal
grandparents. It wasn't a traditional grandparents' house where they lived
in the same place their entire adult life so the home itself held meaning.
They moved constantly. In fact, I'm not sure I can really tell you how long
they stayed in one place. Sometimes their home was a brand-new build on

the lake, and other times they traveled around in a motor home, or we lived with them in a house on the campground they ran for a while. The peace that I found there wasn't in four sturdy walls, but instead in the presence of two sturdy people.

Two people who had expectations and standards, who taught me to follow through with my goals. They had me set the table before dinner and asked my friends to introduce themselves on the phone when they called. There were things that we were absolutely not allowed to do and consequences— although not harsh—for our actions. And because of this, I felt safe. I knew they were the adults, and I was the kid, and therefore, my brain knew to take a break.

My time with my grandparents was like a Norman Rockwell painting— a real-life snow globe where all of the characters were safe and happy and fed.

Outside of this snow globe of safety, I'd learned the opposite: That I was meant to take care of myself. That I needed to self-moderate and motivate. My mother worked so much that she wasn't there to give direction, and my stepfather replaced my name with the insult of the day. I took it upon myself to guide my actions and keep out of trouble. It was—exhausting. Having a haven where someone else was in charge and all I had to do was fall in line felt like someone lifting a stack of books out of my arms and carrying them for me.

I landed safely in the snow globe. My life a perfect picture—my grandfather would go out and pick oranges off the tree and freshly juice them for me in the morning. My grandmother would remind me to take my vitamins. I had someone asking if I'd done my homework, and my grandfather vetted the boys who wanted to spend time with me. It was like the movies I had seen. What I'd imagined other people's childhoods were like.

I lived with them for several months. I made friends. I won an award for leadership. I made straight As. I met a boy. I was thriving.

Then, they instilled a new rule. One that with hindsight seems very simple: come home before the streetlights turn on.

This is reasonable considering we were in Florida, and it's not exactly known for the safety of young girls. I was barely a teenager, and there was no such thing as cell phones for me to use to update them on when I would be back. It was perhaps the most reasonable rule I can imagine. But, for someone who grew up with no rules and no expectations in my day-to-day life, this felt like too much. My snow globe safety bubble had grown bars, and I was suffocating in the prison. So, I called my mom, and the next week I went home.

I gave up fresh-squeezed orange juice, support, safety, friends, and young love because I didn't want to be told what to do. I think that's the complication with authority. When trusted and when safe, it can offer us the comfort we crave. The support that shows us we are not a solitary being out in space without direction or guidance.

Yet, the wounds we carry from figures who wield their authority as weapons make the rules built to keep you safe feel like prisons instead of snow globes.

CHAPTER SEVEN

*

*To the part of you that fears
being trapped in painful emotions.*

INTRODUCTION TO TYPE SEVEN

The Enneagram type seven is commonly referred to as "the enthusiast" or "the epicure." They value freedom, possibility, and positivity. This chapter is dedicated to the part in all of us that fears being trapped in emotional pain. The part that struggles with grief and seeks to distract ourselves from negative emotion. In this chapter, we will address complex elements related to the Enneagram type seven structure, such as:

1. Fearing decision-making

Type sevens have a heightened sense of FOMO (fear of missing out). They want to be where the fun is, because where the fun is, the sad is not. Or, at times, this may not be represented as fun but it can be more subtle and thought of as opportunity. If I take one job, then that closes the door to other jobs, and what if the job I take offers me fewer opportunities than the jobs I pass up? What if I commit to a good relationship only to miss out on a great relationship? Because of this, it can be hard to make decisions. If every decision you make feels a bit like missing out on something else, it can be tempting to stay in limbo—to not decide or to try to do them all at once as a way to keep the options open. Inevitably, this leads to burnout or prevents the type seven from making progress on the things they want to pursue. In order to experience the depth and success they are seeking, type sevens must learn to simplify and give all of their energy to a few things instead of giving little bits away to a lot.

2. Reframing

Type sevens feel an undercurrent of pressure to feel good all the time. Whether that's being happy and positive or living a satisfied life, they feel they must keep their energy up. This can cause them to turn negative experiences into positives or even to downplay and trivialize the trauma they're experiencing. At times, this can be helpful, but when it's used to the extreme, it can invalidate their experience or even cause them to invalidate the experiences of others. The goal for growth in type sevens is not to be happy all the time but instead to honor their emotions equally. To accept and love the negative as much as the positive.

3. Hiding negative emotions

Because of the underlying pressure type sevens carry to be in good spirits, they may keep their negative emotions to themselves. They may feel as though sharing their negativity would be a bummer to the people in their life, they may think they can handle it on their own, or they may even feel pressured to play the role of joy keeper in their community. At other times, they may even be hiding their negative emotions from themselves. This can create a sense of isolation and loneliness when everyone in your life thinks that you are happy even though you are going through so much pain. Others may not know to check in on you because you always seem to be in good spirits. The hope here is that type sevens find a place or two where they can open up about how they are truly feeling so they can receive support from others in their times of need.

4. Seeking joy outside of themselves

When we are running away from negative emotions, we find respite in things that can give us a temporary sense of happiness. We look for distractions in new experiences, shopping, or even drugs or alcohol. Anything that can make the spirits go up and the negative emotions go down. The obvious trouble here is that it's often temporary joy traded in for long-term happiness. Spending all of your money at Target instead of saving for a long and happy retirement. Drinking just one more glass of wine for one more hour of fun, even though it will ruin the entire next day. When type sevens are in their healthiest states, they find their happiness in the here and now. They find joy in the simple things in everyday life. The way the light flows through the window. The laughter of the people they love. When type sevens are grounded and safe, they see that joy is everywhere, and it doesn't have to be made or found—it just is.

5. Doing too much

You can think of type sevens as being on a constant treadmill. Their fear, anxiety, sadness, and grief are running after them, and they keep speeding up as they seek to outrun the things that are threatening to take them down. Because of this fear, they find themselves in constant motion to not have to sit in their pain. They may try to take on every great idea they have. They may commit to too many meetings or go to three parties in one evening so they can leave if things get boring. They may make verbal commitments just to fill their time without feeling obligated to follow through. All of this in fear of sitting still and being sucked down into sadness. This can make the type seven prone to burnout, unlikely to complete their big dreams as they pursue too many at one time, and it can make them flaky with plans as they overcommit to too many people and tasks. Eventually, the goal for type sevens is to simplify. To go deeper into a few areas of interest, relationships, and goals rather than spreading their energy among lots of different things. This will offer them more emotional and even financial support as they make progress on the things they commit their time to, instead of attempting to build fifty bridges with the time and resources they have to complete one.

Although they were written with the type seven structure in mind, these essays and poems are an invitation to explore the part in each of us that struggles with feeling pain. My hope is that they invite you to sit with your grief, give you permission to simplify, and provide you freedom to stay present and find joy where you are.

Happiness as presence.

I've often thought that happiness was a feeling, something blissful and meant to be chased.

An ease of a smile on my cheeks, effortless shining in my eyes, and a buzz felt in my chest—like I awake to life, and life is here for me, and everyone I meet is magic.

As I grew, I learned that happiness isn't the only special thing. That sometimes grief holds magic for you just the same.

That we find ourselves in some of these darker moments, and when we fight for happiness above all, we lose some of the truth of who we are. For me, I believe my seeking of happiness was even the source of much of my suffering.

In the pursuit of happiness, I sacrificed things a bit too early out of fear that they'd bring me down; I made reckless choices all for a temporary feeling at the expense of long-term stability,

And I neglected my ability to have a full range of the human experience.

Then, as I grew in my awareness that the constant pursuit of happiness wasn't serving me, I became neurotic about my resistance to that impulse.

I found myself sinking slowly into my own pain—allowing myself to feel the weight of it, but not using so many of the truly healthy coping skills I'd developed along the way.

Believing that any pursuit of happiness was a failure in my ability to endure my suffering.

Believing that, to win, I must feel my pain and hold it close.

Like a grapefruit, it must be ripped open and eaten delicately, one bleeding segment at a time.

So I writhed, and I waited for something in this to teach me more about what it means to be human and to deepen my connection to life and to others.

I resisted the things that made me feel good and rejected my natural frivolity in hopes of leaving my ego in the dust—

A very sad phoenix rising from my happy ashes.

Until one day it broke, and I knew it was time to find my way back to center—a healthy optimism paired with an acceptance of life's full range of experiences.

And I felt numb.

I googled if I was depressed because I couldn't remember what bliss felt like.

And I journeyed the emotional landscape of average and wondered—
"Is this healthy?"

I'd lived most of my life like a fairy-tale adventure built only for me—I
could be as happy as the risks I was willing to take, and no one could hold
me back.

And then I dove headfirst into the darkness of my soul, which felt
equally as intense as the bliss that I'd known.

But this numbness—this lack of sensation—it felt uncomfortable.
Boring even.

Perhaps scarier even than the darkness had been because this
numbness didn't feel as temporary as I knew the darkness to be. I felt less
alive—which scared me more than pain.

So I asked myself a question that I'd asked a friend before:

"What are the three last moments you remember being truly happy?
What do they have in common?"

For me, it's:

1. Traveling somewhere new—alone.

2. Writing a significant amount every day.

3. Reading more than I felt capable of reading.

And so, I let myself have these things that I enjoyed in ways that I could
enjoy them without sacrificing stability, and I learned to listen to what
makes me happy without neglecting the things that hurt.

Naming and honoring the negative emotions as they arose in my
bones—no fixing. No running. Just allowing.

Now, instead of chasing happiness or coddling my pain, I simply seek
to wake up each day and enjoy it for everything that it is. The beautiful and
messy and incomplete.

Holding the truth that happiness is not found—it is simply being here and fully digesting the beauty of each little moment.

And when happiness is presence—it's not so hard to find. It's in the smell of coffee coming in from the other room, the sound of your child's laughter, the silliness in your own self-doubt, and how amazing it is that our bodies can sometimes feel our emotions before we fully understand them.

Life is a miracle, and I think happiness may be as simple as allowing that to be true.

"I hope you're having a great week."

The day after my dad passed away, I received a well-meaning text, "I hope you're having a great week."

Good intentions sent at the wrong time.

It left my heart pounding, cheeks flushed.

Reminders are everywhere.

"You are not OK."

"You are one of the broken ones."

All of the porcelain boundaries I built to guard a long-wounded heart have started to show their cracks.

And just when I thought that my protection was faltering, it became clear that with these cracks, there becomes a place for the pain to go through and for more love to flow in.

While I'm no longer of the belief that bad things have to happen for good to be made of it, or even that it's our job to make some lemonade from the lemons we are pelted with . . .

I am grateful for the breaking, because it has reminded me of my flesh and bone, of my bleeding humanity, and I can weep more with those who suffer than I was able to before.

More.

For most of my life, when problems needed to be solved, I found my solution in "more." I thought, if I just added more good things in, then I could make a patchwork quilt of good things to cover up all that I was trying to avoid.

When I was in eleventh grade, I'd built my quilt out of extracurricular activities. I joined twelve clubs, played multiple sports, had a job, and was going to my church three days a week. I would go to bed at 2 a.m. and wake up at 6 a.m. to do my homework before another day of school. Eventually, I started to let my grades slip and even walked out of an AP U.S. History test because I hadn't studied. As a teenager, I felt shame. I knew that I'd prioritized the wrong things. I felt judged by my classmates who sat next to me as I seemingly didn't even try to pass this test.

Now that I'm an adult, I can see so clearly that I was avoiding the sadness I felt when I went home. I took any opportunity to occupy my time so that I didn't have to feel the rib-aching heartbreak of being on my own.

The most difficult part of that memory for me is the way I chose to laugh it off. The way I made it seem like I just didn't care about the class instead of asking for the help I needed. I can still see the look of disappointment my classmate gave me, her furrowed brow and wondering eyes. Seemingly saying, "What on earth is wrong with you?" But now I realize they had someone at home to ask them if they'd done their homework, to help them study. Their shock at my behavior was a shock at the way I was laughing it off—not at the fact that I had failed. I was a kid, and I needed help, and my fear of letting anyone know allowed them to take me less seriously than I felt.

As I got older, "more" looked like adding income streams to solve my fear of not making rent, taking every interview for fear of being irrelevant, or going out for drinks with friends every night because I didn't want to be home alone.

The silly thing is that "more" has never loved me well. It has never held me through my pain, only made me the butt of my own jokes. "More" has never sat with me on the floor while I cried or helped me to be brave. Only "less" has done that. Only stopping and saying no and taking time to do nothing. "Less" allowed space for me to be more than the light I thought I had to be. And as I embraced "less," she whispered in my ear, "You—my love—are plenty; you do not need any more."

On meditation.

The first time I tried to meditate, my mind felt like the Gravitron ride at the fair. Thoughts were spinning so quickly they stuck to the sides of my skull.

Sitting still felt like lying on a bed of ants begging me to leap out of my body and onto something better.

I couldn't even be at home by myself, much less in silence with her too.

Eventually, the thoughts turned into ideas that would pile in my mind like freshly washed laundry I didn't have time to put away.

Each thought with their own ticking time bomb of urgency screaming, "If you don't do it now, then someone else will do it first! RUN!"

Then, with time, I learned to watch my thoughts as they passed, as I used to watch the kayakers float down the North Carolina rivers.

Friendly strangers waving as they went on with their day, yet not mine to stop and hold captive in conversation.

Now, some days, my practice allows me to see more of life. To notice the individual moments that build out a day. In this way, I find my joy in the small, the mundane, the ordinary: a sip of coffee, the light on the floor, the synchronicity of seeing a deer and her baby jump from the bushes in the yard.

In these moments, I am able to see my thoughts that used to already be actions before I noticed they were there and stop the ones that are less than helpful.

And yet, on other days, I fidget and squirm as my mind remembers how to spin in its former glory.

On those days, I breathe to get me through. Reminding myself that this is meditation too. One deep breath at a time until we try again tomorrow.

Grief.

I never went to my father's funeral, or my grandfather's, who was more like my father anyway.

I guess I just didn't know what to do there, or perhaps I had other plans.

I was on a plane to Copenhagen the day they laid my grandfather in the ground.

And my dad died the year the world shut down.

They offered to mail me some of his ashes, but I couldn't stand the thought of him burned up, pieced out, and shoved into a Ziploc bag, all so I could have my own kind of closure.

But I still felt cold that I didn't want some, like I was missing a valuable piece of grieving that others seemed to understand.

I wish I'd asked for something that he owned; just something to hold on to that reminded me of him.

I imagine a watch or a journal. Although, by the time he died, he was living with my brother in a trailer where I suppose he didn't have much room for belongings. And he wasn't much of a writer, anyway. I do have letters from him. When I was in elementary school, I would write to him, and he would almost always write back.

"Dad is OK. He misses you. Werking at the lumber yard now. I ain't got much muney but here is sumthing."

I don't know how much I got from my father. His nose, I think; his eyes; and probably his grammar.

Although I started writing stories at a young age and have penned my journals since I was nine, I've always struggled with the rules of writing. My mom would call me after I posted a blog and say, "You know it's 'Joanna and I,' not 'me and Joanna,' right?" I'd act tough like it didn't faze me, and then I'd go make the edits.

Once in therapy, I said, "I've been through a lot, but none of it has fazed me. I just keep going." And in that way, I've lived much of my life like I was skipping the funeral, believing if I keep moving fast enough the pain wouldn't catch up.

Grief continues.

I've had an interesting time allowing myself to express my grief. It feels good to write and to share and to scream when needed. It feels right not to resist the sadness and to allow it to be there with me. And then, out of nowhere, shame will hit me as I remember things I've said or done. A feeling of fear that I'm not actually as strong as I always thought I was, or what if I'm actually just insane? While I know it's not true, the stings of doubt still come in waves. The way I've been able to work through this is to think of friends of mine. If my friend Tina were to go through what I'm experiencing right now, and she behaved like I did, would I think she was crazy or weak? NO. I would think she is feeling and that she is alive. I would think she is making something out of a situation that has no road map and makes no sense. I would see her, and I would love her. Seeing things through that lens helps me to see me and love me in the moments where I feel the least lovable.

Last night, our little family of three went through what our little calls "our memories." He showed us his old artwork and letters to Santa, and my husband and I shared pictures from our childhood. I pulled out a photo of me—my third-grade class photo with a sad smirk on my face—and I realized that little girl did not get a dad who could be there for her, and she grew up strong and self-aware and kind against all odds.

Now, she has to figure out how to grieve an unspeakable and incomprehensible grief, and she's allowed to be messy and loved anyway. I will shield her as she wails; I will stand firm and be open and present and kind as she lowers her productivity, gets angry, gets sad, experiences happiness. Whatever she needs to be right now, she's allowed to be it, because she is loved infinitely, however she's able to show up.

Pain.

Perhaps this is just another part
Of my becoming.

Another brick thrown through my window
Building the foundation of my character.

Perhaps this is just part
Of the process.
Like that time I didn't get my dream job
So I traveled the country instead.

Or maybe this is just a bad thing—to be felt.
A stab unexplained—no purpose or meaning.

Another wound to be tended
Not to be so trivialized as to be assigned a purpose.

Like the man who emailed me for four years after two mediocre dates.
Uncertain of whether he loved me or hated me.
So he chose to hurt me just in case.
As to whether he loved me or hated me
So, he chose to hurt me just in case.

You see, sometimes pain . . . it has meaning
And sometimes it just has to be felt.

Tears.

What if tears are just your heart sweating
After all of its hard work?

Time.

My heart is an engine running.
Clock ticking.
A ticktock reminder that life is fleeting.

I can feel the stampede heartbeat
Of all I want to do
And be
And see.

A rumbling pressure
To keep pace with life
Running breathless side by side.

But
This year I realized that
I've never seen the leaves grow on the trees before.
They seem to shift from barren brown to green tipped giants into lush
green walls
In what feels like a single breath.

So now each day, I check the trees
And look for signs of new growth, and
Though this won't get me where I'm going any faster
I'm not sure there's anywhere else I'd rather go.

Seeking versus being.

Seeking joy outside of ourselves is like
Being a dehydrated traveler crawling in search of water in the desert
    while ignoring the canteen on our back.

A partner's perspective.

I used to wonder how he was singing in the shower
When I was still picking my heart up off the floor. But Steinbeck wrote
    that people sing the most beautiful songs when they're sad.
So maybe he felt it more than I knew.

Loneliness in joy.

My husband asked me yesterday if there's anything going on underneath my
demeanor. He's learned oftentimes I just go about life as usual and hold my
pain in some secret compartment I only access when forced.

He said, "I can see you're doing a lot of things that bring you joy, and I just want to check in and make sure I'm not missing something." It was fascinating to me because I have felt darker than usual and didn't even realize I'd been expressing joy.

This is a phenomenon I see in lots of other type sevens. When we're gathered together and just experiencing one another's brightness and someone asks, "What's going on in your life right now?" There is often an overflow of burdens we're carrying that can't be felt in our light demeanor.

This has been my greatest loneliness in life. Not knowing how to be seen in my darkness and, therefore, handling my struggles in private. This has left me, at times, in a room full of people who love me but feeling completely alone.

This season of life is a holding of both pain and joy without resistance.

I've learned to hold my pain without struggling to get free, and my joy permeates through my bone marrow.

In some ways, this is an exciting time in my life. I am emerging, strengthening, and clarifying. I feel more connected to the sacred and to my purpose.

And it hurts.

That's OK too.

My mind.

My mind is an airport terminal.
Long hallways pointing in every direction, each a new
Possibility—a potential destination.

When I was younger, I would hop on a plane
And embrace whatever we found there.
Sometimes heartache.
Sometimes adventure.
Often broke.

Now, it's more complicated.
There are others in tow and more
Baggage to carry.

Two perfectly good flights
Going in opposite directions pull at my roller bags
While I sit knees to chest—frozen
On the moving walkway.

There are no guarantees that I will
Take the right plane.
No promises of a successful landing.

Yet, we both know I can't stay in this airport
Forever, so eventually I must board, and even
Though my heart may pound in response to the
Plane it longs to catch—my mind keeps
Staring down the hallways wondering
If taking the plane I most want will mean missing my only chance.

CONCLUSION

To the part in each of us learning to live with pain.

I almost always sleep with my hair in braids. I actually started doing this when I was bedridden for about three weeks in 2019. I didn't have the physical energy to fix my hair, and if put into a bun every day, my curls would get matted and knotted at the crown of my head.

I'd wiped the origin of this habit from my memory. Believing that it started as a stylistic choice. I ended up liking what it does to my waves, and it takes less time than styling it.

But it came out of my loss.

Years later, as I still manage the aftermath of whatever was happening to my body, I am continually reminded of my new normal.

Some days, I forget, and other days—like the day that I am writing this to you—my lungs are tight, and I cough myself to sleep.

We aren't taught to talk about these things. I wasn't prepared to live with these things. The brashness that comes with living in pain. The loss of energy that comes from feeling disconnected from my own body. The tears that come out of nowhere.

The easy overwhelm.

My comfort with pain has grown, but I was prepared for being in pain, not as much for living in pain.

There's a clear difference here. Being in pain is something that happens, and it leaves feeling like something I can control. Living in pain is something that requires my full acceptance.

It's just that pain has always felt like a choice, both for myself and for others. My mentality was: if I'm feeling pain, then I must be choosing to focus on it.

The story that I must make gold out of ashes is a story I lived with for life, and at times, it served me well. But I finally feel safe enough to open up to the fact that sometimes ashes are just fucking ashes and they suck and they're here and it's not my job to pretend like they're gold hiding in ashes' clothing.

It's likely that gold will come of these things because the universe is a vast and magical place. But I am worthy, my pain is worthy, my life is worthy— even if it doesn't—and that acceptance makes all the difference.

CHAPTER EIGHT

*

*To the part of you that feels
it must be strong.*

INTRODUCTION TO TYPE EIGHT

The Enneagram type eight is commonly referred to as "the challenger." They value making their own choices, protecting themselves from harm, and getting justice for the underdog. This chapter is dedicated to the part in all of us that guards the part of us we fear will be hurt. The part that pretends to be strong even when we feel weak and resists being controlled by others. In this chapter we will address complex elements related to the enneagram type eight structure, such as:

1. Fear of betrayal

The jury is still out about whether our Enneagram type forms in childhood or if we are born with a predisposition to certain fears and motivators. However, we do have childhood experiences that solidify our type structure. For type eights, that's the memory of an early betrayal, a realization that the people you thought you could trust are not who you thought they were. In adulthood, this can lead type eights to keeping their vulnerabilities and their softness close to their chest for fear of it being used against them. The hope is that eventually the type eight will develop safe and trustworthy relationships that allow them the space to let that guard down and be supported by others.

2. Denial

When type eights feel negative emotions like anxiety, sadness, or even just vulnerability, their go-to protective response is denial. This can look like denying the existence of the thing that's making them uncomfortable or simply downplaying the importance of it. They may become defensive if challenged on this and/or never even tell you that they've chosen to ignore the feelings at all. This mechanism leads to ignoring physical ailments until they've gotten far worse than they had to be. It can look like downplaying the importance of someone else's concern that has been brought up to them. The work is in getting comfortable with acknowledging their humanity. Admitting to themselves it's OK to feel weak at times and to communicate from a place of vulnerability instead of strength.

3. Focus on justice

More than any other type structure, type eights scan for inequities. They pay close attention to leadership and how the leadership is treating those who aren't as able to defend themselves. They seek fairness and justice in all things. Additionally, because type eights tend to see themselves as indestructible, they are likely to put themselves on the line for those who they deem need their protection.

4. Pushing past their limits

In a similar lane as denial, type eights push themselves past their limits, even thinking they have no limitations at times. They hold themselves to extremely high standards of production, physical strength, and emotional toughness. They value their ability to be resilient to the extent that they don't allow adequate rest and recuperation. This can lead to burnout, sickness, and serious injury. The art of learning to respect their limitations is incredibly important for learning where to set appropriate boundaries with themselves and others.

Although they were written with the type eight structure in mind, these essays and poems are an invitation to explore the part in each of us that seeks to hide our vulnerability. My hope is that they invite you to experience deep rest and allow yourself to sit with the parts you're afraid of getting hurt.

On big reactions.

> Triggers are children hiding under the bed waiting to jump out when you graze your feet by the dust cover.
> You know they're there, but somehow it still surprises you when they leap.

> Nails digging into my palms, chest tight, shoulders to ears tense.

> I get firm and definitive.

> No.
> Never.
> Always.
> Will not.
> Cannot.

My soul seems to run faster than my body, and I flee toward the door
   trying to just catch up.

Others, they yell—begging to be seen.
Like a child facing a bear, arms stretched over head—growling—trying
   to make themselves seem bigger than they feel.

I am sad that we've trivialized such a delicate word—"triggered"
   sounds like watered-down whiskey used to define feeling any sort
   of discomfort.

It is not so soft as whiskey and water

It's Jack Daniels neat—so cheap and potent that it burns.

And I think sometimes we assume that our reactions should be softer
   because they're ancient.
Responding to the pain of our childhood more than our immediate
   surroundings.

But
Isn't that why it burns so much?
They are the wounds we built when we were softest to the touch.

Like Play-Doh molded and shaped and left out in the sun,
The cracks of our begging to be loved
Crumble under the weight of being told they're too much.

And big feelings generate big reactions that seem far from appropriate
for the time.

If I could, I would kiss the apples of our embarrassed cheeks to
remind them that they are safe, that they are loved, and that
this impossible feeling, though large as it seems, will be a distant
memory of a moment if allowed to just be enough.

On learning to trust love.

I put my own suitcase in the car today—
Something I don't have to do often—and thought, "Does he love me so
well it makes me weak?"

For years, love was a barbed wire fence I had to climb alone.
Getting nicked and scratched and sometimes jolted.
Carrying myself through the trenches for fear of sinking lifelessly into
the mud.

But this is not the house of my childhood.
Here it is warm, and love is served fresh baked.
Here—strength isn't my savior
But vulnerability that makes me safe.

On learning not to choose force.

The iron in your blood flows heavy with the weight of inequity.

At times, a wrecking ball swinging at the structures mitigating the safety of yourself and others.

At others, a gate standing guard against anyone wanting in or out for fear of being hit from behind.

Neither objectively bad when used in the right timing. A wrecking ball or a fence can be useful when in danger. But where do they fit when all is well?

A wrecking ball is not helpful in a room of fragile things, such as feelings of tenderness and welcome, a shattering of safety where it meant to protect.

A fence is not helpful when you're left fending for yourself, a wall keeping love out that it meant to keep in.

It is beautiful, the iron that pumps through your veins, a sign of the care that you possess.

It's just that, perhaps forming that iron into a container is more appropriate when the fragile mess of being human just needs to be held.

On speaking up at the wrong time.

One of my less favorable qualities is that I can argue about anything. I'd like to tell you it's a skill, but it's more of a delusion. I decide where I stand on something and dig my heels in until we both die. I didn't realize this was something I do until I got married to my now husband. It's probably because he does it too, and if we didn't wake up to it, we'd die together of exhaustion, holding hands with our mouths pursed in preparation for, "Well, actually . . ."

In the late summer of 2010, I took a backpacking trip across Europe with my ex-husband and his brother. We flew into Rome, spent some time on the coast of Italy, took a train to Paris, to Zurich, to Edinburgh, and ended in London. It was the trip of my dreams, and honestly, it sucked. We were three people with three very different needs and travel styles who couldn't find a healthy compromise. We had limited funds with differing views on how we should spend our money. They were brothers, and we were married, so my partner had to play the bridge between the two most important relationships in his life. I wanted to explore alone, and that scared him, and his desire to keep me nearby made me feel smothered and controlled. It looked like a grand adventure from the outside, but inside, I was waking up to the fact that the person I'd married only a year prior just didn't get me at all.

One exhausting night in Paris, we were hungry, broke, and sitting along the Seine on these trampolines that the city had put up. This could have been a respite in the experience, but *my* argumentative ass had unexpressed needs, and they came out SIDEWAYS. My brother-in-law brought up a documentary he'd watched about Louis Vuitton and how someone else was designing for them. Here's the thing about my particular brand of argumentative: I don't have to be confident that I am the most informed on the topic. I just find something I feel confident about, and we run with that arrogance all the way to the depths of the earth. So, while this sweet human was telling me that he'd literally done the research of watching this documentary, I felt in my gut like I knew something about this, and so

I argued the point with him. Insistent that it wasn't true until we both got so angry, and my partner got so uncomfortable, that we walked in three opposite directions, and I finally got the alone time I'd been begging for.

I didn't intend to get into an argument with my brother-in-law. I adored him and still do, but I had felt shut down, ignored, treated as irrational, and controlled the entire trip, and this was the moment for me to be heard . . . even if it was about the exact wrong thing.

This argument is one of those memories that still makes me shiver when I think about it. It was a conversation where I let my arrogance take over and ruin what could have been a nice time. An argument that now would've easily been solved with a quick Google search on our phones turned into hours of tension.

Here's the thing though, it wasn't about the designer, was it? It was about the weeks of unmet needs. About feeling ignored. About not having confidence to put my foot down when it mattered but having endless confidence when it didn't.

On the beauty of being honest.

There is no back-peddling in poetry.
No overexplaining.
No take-backs.

There isn't room for people-pleasing—
Positive-thinking qualifiers.

It is only you, your honesty, and the breath of that moment. A required honoring of however you are experiencing it today.

And perhaps that's why we need poetry.
To honor our truth no matter how messy.
To hold space for the bright without
Reminding ourselves that there is also dark.
Witnessing the grief without forcing it into a purpose.

In poetry, the moments just are.
We can't manipulate them to comfort our human sensibilities.
Poetry asks us to sit with things, honor them, and allow them to just be.

And therein lies its magic.

On respecting your limitations.

I hear you say, "I don't have limitations."
But I wonder where you learned that rest is only meant for the broken.

When are you allowed to say, "This is too much!"
Because it's amazing the things we can live through when we think we
    have to strive—
But I wonder if your tolerance is higher than it was ever supposed
    to be.

And I can't help thinking of you as a little kid.

Wide-eyed

And open

Needing to know that you will be taken care of.

All to be shown that only the strong survive.

And I wonder what your body is trying to tell you, although it's subtle
   at best—

Will you listen to its whispers, or will it have to scream for you to rest?

On being the strong one.

My heart is the Mexican sunflower my neighbor planted this spring, caged
up in hopes of keeping it safe as it stretches its leaves trying to reach the sun.

In the mornings when I get into my car, I often think it looks like it
should be set free. But I worry that someone will take a weedwacker to
its base or hack at it in the winter when the blooms are gone—mistaking
something beautiful and tender for a weed just because its roots look
so strong.

She planted it away from the other flowers across the gravel drive with
hopes of improving what was once a lackluster bed of grass.

I just wonder if the sunflower knows that's why it's set apart? If it
realizes that it needs that south-facing sun—bright and hot—a kind of heat
that would wither other petals. Or does it think it was just too much for the
other flowers to love?

Layered feelings.

Yesterday, I planted a garden
And I was busy.
So busy that I forgot about my sadness.

I thought for a bit—
Maybe I should stay busy until
The darkness goes away.

But then I remember it's OK to be sad
And it's not a shame to want to be happy
And it's not very nice to call yourself
Dramatic just because you have layered feelings.

And today I love this espresso that I'm sipping
And the azaleas are dancing for me
And I am sad.

I am scared and I feel powerless against so much pain
That seems to be everywhere I look.

And I remembered the time I smiled at a stranger
And she lit up like fireworks coursed through her veins
And it felt like that game we used to play as children.
The one where you pretend to crack an egg on your friend's head.

Warm and comforting and silly.

There is pain coursing through the roots of our systems.
And humanity is still so beautiful I could burst.

On comfort in chaos.

My least favorite life lesson so far has been the importance of short-term
sacrifice in order to ensure long-term comfort. Learning the importance
of a savings account, health insurance, and regularly going to the dentist.
Things that feel dull, stressful, or even life-sucking, some would say. All
in the awareness that shoveling out money, time, and energy now will put
us in less situations qualified as a crisis later on. The trouble with learning
this lesson is that I was, and always have been, quite comfortable in a
crisis. In fact, I may even be more comfortable in a crisis than in the calm.
I know what to do in a crisis. Crisis raised me. High heart rates, shortened
breath, quick problem-solving, keeping my eyes out for threats. Easy
stuff. Breathing deeply, feet on the ground, silence—that's a panic attack
waiting to happen. What is this strange and unfamiliar feeling, and when is
someone going to blow this up?

Ironically, I became very good at blowing up my own peace so that no
one else could. Filling my schedule to the brim, finding things to be upset
about, digging my heels down in fights to make sure I see them at their
angriest before I get too comfortable. Turns out, when you are raised in
chaos, you become quite comfortable there, and anything else feels a bit like
walking on a tightrope 10,000 feet above the ground, knowing that at any

moment someone could pull the trampoline out from under you and there's nothing you could do about it.

Humans are funny this way. We can find anything to feel shame about. I think it happens because we just don't have enough to do. Compared to our ancestors, I mean. Cavemen didn't have time to stress about whether they were giving their kids too much processed food. They were busy trying to stay alive. In a way, this absurd obsession with improving everything comes from our comfort. Our cells don't realize that we aren't in constant threat, so they look for the threats all around. Some days, the threat is our workload, and other days, the threat is the fact that we seem to be relaxing somehow and that can't be right. *Alert*Alert*Alert* And all of a sudden, while we're relaxing in a mall Barnes & Noble enjoying our day off, we can't quite find our breath, and we pick a fight with our partner about the way they fold the towels. Just me?

Even if you're not obsessed with towel tidiness, you know what I'm talking about though, don't you? The moment where everything seems to be good and we're finally getting a break, something in our brain clicks and tells us to check our emails, ask our partner a question that will inevitably pick a fight, look for evidence that we are actually not as OK as we happen to feel in this moment.

I get it, a very real part of us is wired for self-defense. When we're on vacation or just happy, that part sort of loses its job, and I don't expect it to go down quietly. It's quite directly wired to do anything but that.

On hiding vulnerability.

There's a bump on my right ring finger where my pen rests.
A souvenir from going to battle with my heart.

It sits against the scar on my middle finger
Of the same hand.
A Nike Swoosh–shaped memory of playing
Hide-and-seek with a metal shed for base.

There is a scar on my left foot
From jumping off of a roof
And landing barefooted onto a
Piece of shattered concrete.

My favorite is along my left thumb.
A faded line where I took a saw to my bone at five.

We bandaged it up with toilet paper and Scotch Tape
And I tried not to cry for fear of being called sensitive.

My fingers are still pinpricked from days picking tomatoes—
Twenty-five cents a bucket, sunburned shoulders, and free childcare for
    my overworked mother.

Evenings were spent sorting the tomatoes—my job was to pull out the
    bad ones and the men would hand me large ripe ones with a little
    bit of salt, and we'd eat them like apples even though I didn't really
    care for tomatoes—
I didn't want to be called picky.

Origin.

I remember all too well
The need to tiptoe.

Like a dancer in a field of mines
I tried to make something beautiful out of fear.

And I hate the way loud sounds
Still make me sit up straight
Chills and sorrow stiffening my spine.

I hate how disapproving looks still
Feel like a ruler on the wrist
And even though I've not seen you in decades
Every loud noise reminds me that you exist.

I remember all too well the need to tiptoe.
So much that sometimes I can't tell
Wildflowers from bombs.

CONCLUSION

To the part in each of us that is still learning to accept our limitations.

The other day, I had to come home from work because I was exhausted. I pulled into the parking lot, and I realized I wasn't going to be able to show up that day. I'd spent the week pushing myself past my physical and emotional limits, and my body told me, "No more."

You might think that I went home and took a nap or let myself rest, but I decided that my time off would be earned by cleaning out my patio garden. I would carry large tubs full of heavy dirt across the yard and clean them out as my penance for not being able to work.

As I carried my third bin down the hill, it felt like someone had taken an ice pick to my head, and I crashed to my knees. The entire right side of my skull was throbbing in pain. I'd gotten the second migraine of my life. It's as if my body tried to tell me calmly, but I didn't listen, and so she had to scream. I don't know about you, but sometimes for me, the standard for which I expect myself to perform just keeps rising and rising. The pressures boiling in from all sides, all self-imposed but equally intense. Weakness is not allowed in the workplace, in relationships, even in the way we do our hobbies. Even rest can be something to conquer.

At times, the feeling of being capable is invigorating and affirming. Other times, the expectations I've created for myself feel like an anvil tied to my ankle.

After years of being capable, people begin to expect you to show up a certain way and perform your duties as you always have. And just like that you become the person that others look to when something needs to be handled.

But wouldn't it be nice sometimes to lay your head in the arms of someone stronger? To be told that it's safe to close your eyes and rest and to have the trust to believe them? There is no lesson in this today because I think we all know we should do less. But, right now, I just want to grieve the life you could have had if all had gone well. The sense that it will be taken care of and it's not yours to handle. To grieve the version of you that got to be "go with the flow" because someone else did the work that you are doing now. Someone else kept it all under control.

CHAPTER NINE

*

*To the part of you that feels
it must be easy to get along with.*

INTRODUCTION TO TYPE NINE

The Enneagram type nine is most often referred to as "the peacemaker." They fear loss of connection and seek to preserve their own peace of mind. This chapter is dedicated to the part in all of us that is afraid to speak up. The part that loses sight of yourself in pursuit of making others comfortable.

1. Avoiding conflict

With losing connection as a major fear and peace of mind as their priority, conflict is clearly a concern for type nines. The fear of this can be intense enough that they may quiet their preferences, shove down the things that bother them, or even try to eliminate their needs. The trouble is that, in essence, our type nines are in the heart of the anger triad. Meaning they have a fire internally that is burning whether they express it or not. This fire can often come out in passive-aggressive ways or at times it may erupt like a volcano after they've silenced themselves for long enough. The practice is learning that people will still remain even if they express themselves honestly over time.

2. Merging

In attempts to resist separation, type nines may find that they merge in relationships, adopting the personality traits and preferences of the people they spend the most time with. This can be an incredible asset, as they make other people feel comfortable to be themselves, but the trouble is that in this process they may lose sight of who they are. It's important for type nines to spend time alone out of their house to regain a sense of relationship to their independence and knowledge of who they are.

3. Feeling as though it's best if they don't exist

The childhood wound of a type nine is the belief that everything would be better if they didn't exist. That their presence is so stressful that they should make themselves as small as possible to avoid making rifts. With this as an origin story it is no wonder that type nines may find themselves asking more questions than giving answers, frequently self-forgetting, and even going through entire relationships without truly feeling seen and known. At the core of growth work for the Enneagram type nine is the belief that their presence in its absolute fullness matters and makes a difference.

4. Numbing to life

As the fear of things disrupting their peace of mind grows, type nines may start to resist any intense emotion. Good or bad. They may numb to the overstimulation of their environment and zone out as an attempt not to feel overwhelmed or stressed out. They may numb through watching TV, scrolling on social media, or even playing golf. This numbing to life may maintain an illusion of peace for the type nine, but it also stands in the way of their ability to fully embrace the depth of all that being human has to offer. Both the depths of joy and pain that—when shared—ultimately creates the connections the type nine is seeking to preserve.

Although they were written with the type nine structure in mind, these essays are an invitation to explore the part in each of us that seeks to make ourselves as inoffensive as possible. My hope is that they invite you to live a life in full vibrancy.

Agreeable.

To the parts of us that feel as though we have to blend in to be loved. The parts that hear a rift when we speak up. The ones that can't quite master the art of interjecting for fear of being too much. You were never made to be invisible. This fire in your gut is meant to light up the world around you, not burn you from the inside out.

You offer us more than your silence.

And, of course, there is nothing wrong with being intentional with your words.

But I wonder how many times you leave a party and wonder if anyone really noticed you were there.

And how many times you start a sentence only for someone else to drown out the sound, and does it hurt when you realize that your closest friends don't even really quite know you?

You offer us more than your silence.

We fall in love with your disruption. Your chaos is invigorating.

And all those years of listening have made you wiser than you probably know.

Hippy town.

I live in a hippy town.

A tourist destination for the energetically curious. There's an interesting phenomenon that you can watch from café windows.

When people come to visit, they will often dress in boho or hippy-style clothing. Hundred-dollar skirts meant to look like they were purchased at a thrift store. Perfectly groomed hair with a feather clipped in. It's obvious to us the tourists playing hippy for a day and those who have made it a lifestyle. The true hippies who live in our town wear their sacrifices on their skin. They smell of earth and sunshine and have dirt under their nails from digging up breakfast. Those playing hippy smell like Bloomingdale's wearing a gardener's clothes.

It reminds me of the times I've played tourist in my own skin. The versions of me that I played just so I could blend in.

The ease of which I put on an opinion or a personality as a way not to vibrate at too large a frequency as to make rifts in the space between myself and others. A visitor in my own body watching my soul sink back as my desire to connect took the lead.

Blending my being with the surrounding—a whisper of someone easy to get along with.

In meditation, we often chant "om." Recently, I came to understand that it's a representation of joining our self with the entirety of the universe. An honoring of the self, the expanse of time, and of all people. In many ways, playing tourist in this life gives us a chance to experience a watered-down version of "om," to see what it's like to be in another's shoes. It's a beautiful invitation into seeing ourselves not as separate from others, but as deeply and intrinsically connected. However, when blending leads to self-forgetting, "om" cannot truly occur. It is joining self with the expanse of the universe—which we cannot truly do when self is not present.

Playing tourist can be a way in which we understand the beauty and the struggle of others. Yet, as visitors, we only mimic the experiences of those we surround ourselves with. We leave unscarred and without dirt beneath our nails. An illusion of connection that doesn't require sacrifice. As we seek to stand fully in our purpose, to be more than a vacant body designed to fit in, we must risk wearing life on our skin. The scars and the aches of trying and failing. The pains of rejection and loss. This is where we go from merging into "om." When self is fully developed, and others are understood still—no longer tucking away our depths but allowing both to exist at once.

When we are tempted to blend in a moment, we should radiate—may we whisper, "I love you," back into our bones and drink of the courage to stand in "om."

Growing pains.

We don't talk much about growing pains.

How focusing on improving our life or rewiring our old coping mechanisms can sometimes feel worse than just living into the behaviors that are most comfortable.

We champion personal growth and encourage self-reflection, yet we neglect to acknowledge that it sometimes aches. Like beginning to work out again after weeks of taking a break, it's sore as the muscles tear and reform.

At times, growth is choosing the more difficult path. It's doing things that feel unnatural until they become our new normal. It's taking care of our future happiness in exchange for our momentary satisfaction.

I don't care what anyone says—spending money is more fun than saving money. It just is. But it's also a recipe for a lifetime of feeling like you are underwater.

So, yes, it's worth it. But it's definitely not as much fun.

I think it's important that we talk about this, because so much of self-help work is all "Love and light and follow your bliss," and "When it's right, it's easy," but I want to challenge that idea.

Sometimes, when it's right, it's hard.

It's hard because it's an unflexed muscle, a path that's never been walked before and the briars haven't been cleared away yet.

It's moving away from what is easy and choosing to do what is right for us even when it's hard.

Songbirds.

No one tells the songbirds that there are plenty of songs being sung—and we don't see a field of flowers and think they're all great except one.

I have never heard a symphony with just one too many members—yet, you think there are so many voices that yours no longer matters.

I understand that it is risky to make a point to stand out. How do you know you won't be targeted or guarantee you won't hurt somebody else?

And the truth is that I can't promise you those things will not happen. You will get hurt, and you will hurt someone, and you will be alive. For as long as you use your silence as a shield, the truth of who you are will go undervalued.

That sensation that you feel when it seems like no one really gets you—it comes from hiding the depths of who you are under the mask of "I'm easygoing."

It's in those messy moments when you piss somebody off and then you sit together, and you struggle until you figure something out. That's the kind of staying that actually tells you that you are loved—because they're here for all of your messiness—not just for how much you don't speak up.

And for those who liked you better when your mouth was sewn shut—I wonder how they benefited from you feeling like you're not enough? Because the people who will love your fullness and your flaws—they're real, and they're ready whenever you are.

Secret feelings.

I spent most of my life with my body doing what it was supposed to do. Functioning like a machine that never needed repairs.

Then in 2019, I came down with a mysterious sickness. Body aches, difficulty breathing, and extreme fatigue to the point where I could barely walk to the bathroom for three weeks. The sickness turned to pneumonia, and over two years later, I am still navigating the impact.

To have a foreign substance inside my lungs. It feels like aliens are inside my body. Like I've betrayed myself.

I've spent all of these years learning how to love this body well, and like a scorned lover, I feel betrayed by it giving up on me.

Not to mention the difficulty I had navigating the medical system. Insurance being more expensive than paying out of pocket, but paying out of pocket was still adding up. A different doctor for every part of my body and it seemed like no one was talking with one another. I grew fragile and exhausted appointment after appointment, scan after scan, bill after bill.

Although—I will say—one bright spot of this experience was paying attention to the decorations the different receptionists use behind their desks and eavesdropping on their conversations.

Eavesdropping is one of my absolute favorite pastimes. My husband gives me a hard time because I'm not even good at it. We'll go out to eat, and I'll just start listening to someone else's conversation, and he'll have to tell me that I'm staring. But you hear so much good stuff when you eavesdrop. You can gauge how a first date is going, get a sneak peek into the complex dynamics of a marriage, pick up on some parenting dos or parenting don'ts.

Once 2020 hit, we isolated intensely because of the high risk involving my lungs. We didn't go to the grocery store or the coffee shop. We didn't go out to eat. The only place I engaged with other people was at doctors' offices or the hospital. As you could imagine, this severely limited my eavesdropping opportunities. In fact, we were down to my household, which mostly consisted of discussing *The Legend of Zelda: Breath of the Wild*. So the doctors' offices were my one opportunity to get my fix, my chance at picking up anything of interest.

Pairing eavesdropping with observing the decor people choose to represent themselves was the only bright spot of going to so many different doctors' offices. What did they choose to hang up to express their personality? For some, it was drawings from a lover. One receptionist must have married a tattoo artist, because he would draw her these roses that seemed like I'd seen them in a tattoo book before. Others had pictures of their kids or their birthday banner from two months prior. The most memorable so far had runner's tags, glitter banners, and lots of signs saying, "If you can't shine, then sparkle."

This particular day, I was already dangling feetfirst about to jump out of the medical care airplane and just fend for myself. Feeling hopeless and confused about what was going on with my body and anxious about catching Covid, which felt like a death sentence at the time. I walked into the office two minutes before my appointment. It turns out, at this doctor's office two minutes early was actually twenty-eight minutes late. I was supposed to be there thirty minutes early. They cancelled my appointment.

It felt like the stress of every single hospital gown, stethoscope, CT scan—every poke and every prod—swelled into emotions that I didn't even realize had started coming out of my eyes. I was shaking and sobbing, and I could barely stand. Of course, I was embarrassed and uncomfortable. I felt like a child pitching a fit in the grocery store looking for her mother. But I didn't seem to have much choice over my reaction or my own body.

The receptionist with glitter on the walls and painted across her eyes clearly felt bad for me. So, in what was an act of kindness in her mind, she grabbed my hand and placed a little coin in my palm.

I can understand how she thought what she was doing was kind, but to me, it felt like a death sentence. I'd spent all year not coming in contact with even the people I love, most because of the buckling awareness that there is a rapidly spreading disease that I was uniquely qualified to die from. So, to have a random woman violate my space like that felt horrifying and not at all comforting.

I smiled at her because, like a good little girl, I didn't want to make her uncomfortable, and I put my head down, walked to my car, sobbed in private, and for the next two weeks, I waited for any sign of a fever or a cough.

Angry poetry.

I used to speak up less.
I'd hold my tongue when someone stepped on my toes or the toes of
 another.
The blood seeping from that muscle as my teeth dug deeper.
Better to harm myself than to make my oppressor feel uncomfortable.
When my gut learned to speak, it behaved like a child learning to use
 ChapStick for the first time.
I rolled my defensiveness all the way up and made a mess of it.
The years of silencing my difficulty, the years of trying to be smaller.
It makes it easy to confuse someone taking advantage of others with
 someone just having a powerful presence.
I've searched eyes for what was left behind in their mother's womb.
Intuition, emotional complexity, deep wells of compassion.
It's been a while since I've written an angry poem.
I used to write them often.
Shouting rhythmic suppression from my gut like a fountain pen
 overflowing.
While maybe not wise or calculated or particularly intentional,
There are moments when angry poetry feels like the only option.

Invisibility.

Have you ever felt the ache of a sentence left unheard?

When this happens to me, it's like someone yanks me at my collar, and we warp back to childhood. A kid among chaos getting lost in the crowd.

The tantrum under my stinging tear ducts wanting someone just to notice I'm there—to clock my lack of contribution and remind me that I am not invisible.

As a child, being invisible was an art form—wrapping the cloak around my shoulders hiding my needs and existence as everyone else seemed to need more.

And the pain that it caused felt manageable compared to the fear that they would leave. Yet at some point, the cloak begins to hide us even from ourselves. As others seem so clear in picture, our wants and needs grow pixelated.

It can feel as though speaking up is pants too tight.
Zipped up with a bulging heart spilling over the top.
A laced-up mouth with eyes begging for a listening ear.

But relationships are a tangled mess of triggers
Where each long to be heard and seen
The unhealed wounds of our childhood silencing some and
Causing others to scream.

Isolation is less lonely than a bid for connection dismissed
And the journal never says it's not a good time.
So, the pen flows freely on a book running out of pages—
A constant ear when your throat feels closed up.

Finding our voice.

I moved into my first solo apartment when I was twenty-eight years old.
No roommates, no partner, no one to tell me what I should and shouldn't
do with my space. One of the first decisions I made was not to have any
houseplants. I didn't want to be responsible for them, and quite frankly, I
didn't want to intentionally bring buckets of dirt into my house. It felt weird
to me. It was about six months after I moved in that I started showing my
boyfriend (now husband) photos of spaces I really loved, and he lightly
offered that the thing they all had in common were tons and tons
of houseplants. I'd collected images of very blank homes with hundreds of
beautiful houseplants. He mentioned that maybe I did like houseplants,
after all.

I, of course, denied it and resisted every time he offered that I pick one
up. Eventually, he gifted me an air plant to hang from my window. No dirt.
Low responsibility. It was the perfect gateway plant.

After a while, that air plant became an air plant and a succulent, and then eventually an air plant, a succulent, and a cactus. By the time my husband and I moved in together, we had a solid collection of ten or so low-maintenance plants I adored.

In 2020, when the world shut down, I was fully immersed in my new hobby and filled our home with pothos and snake plants and philodendrons. I created a routine to care for them, and I was a full-on plant hoarder. I learned to propagate. I repotted when the roots were too much for their container. I fertilized, and I paid meticulous attention to their every change in color.

What I wasn't prepared for was all of the cutting away I'd have to do. Leaves that would turn brown or yellow seemed like a death sentence to a plant in my mind. It was as if, once it had hit that point, the life cycle must be over. But many times, it just needed to be clipped away so the healthy leaves could continue thriving.

Sometimes the plant just needed a new environment, and the early leaves that browned were warning signs of the change that the plant would need.

I think that's what they don't tell you about growth—that there is so much that has to be cut away in order for things to thrive.

In many ways, a major part in spurring growth is the same in humans as in plants. Recognizing when a leaf is dead and separating it from the rest, sometimes changing its environment.

In the same way—as we grow and change in our life and start to use our voice or finally speak up for ourselves—there will inevitably be people who wither around our newfound strength. People who were drawn to us because of our tendency to please. People who preferred us as the givers and not the ones with need.

When this happens, we may be tempted to wither—to shrink back—
to make our needs silent again in the hope that they can grow in proximity
to us. However, this is the moment to remember the pothos, to clip away
the withering ties that demand that we stay small. This is the moment to
welcome a new environment with plenty of sunshine, where we can enjoy
the company that prefers us healthy and full and alive.

Knowing that you matter.

The coals to the fire in your belly are still glowing, and
As much as you try to starve them of oxygen, they keep catching flame.

Perhaps you think they're meant to be hidden—
That others will be burned in their presence.

But there are people in your life begging just to keep warm in your light.

And I know that there are times that you've set the fire free and
It wasn't well received.

But I wonder if, perhaps, you were shining for the wrong audience?

Or

Maybe a little glow every day is less hot than a raging fire after so much
time being suffocated?

And when you wonder if your presence even matters,
I ask you to remember the last time you felt the healing fires of
    someone's warmth.
How invigorating it is to see someone stand in their truth and own their
    space.

And to remember that, more than most, you see the bleeding wounds
    of those rejected
Because they are healed by those—like you—with kind and wild hearts
    showing up fully as they are.

CONCLUSION

To the part in each of us that fears showing up.

As I began my review process of this book, I started to feel as though I'd
dealt my mother a bad hand. I wrote of the ways in which she's impacted
me negatively but felt as though I didn't express as much about the things
that are incredible about her. I suppose that happens when what you're
writing about is a system designed to expose our childhood wounds.

At first, I considered taking out specifics and making things vaguer, but
then I realized that my mother is here so much because she was there. She
showed up.

My father wounded me with his absence. His inability to defeat his demons. The way he withdrew from life even before he chose to die.

But my mother wounded me with her choice to be there. To try over and over again, and messing up like humans do. But she was present and available, and she fought for us every single day.

Both parents left scars—as all of us who become parents inevitably do—but there is only one parent I call when all feels lost.

Because she is fully there.

And as I think about my own parental journey, it can be tempting to pull back and disengage. To give less so I make fewer mistakes.

There are times when I know I've said or done the wrong thing, and I'm learning to say sorry and to try better next time instead of exiting the space.

To sit with the pain of my son's big emotions. Not to get overwhelmed at his disappointment. To stay in my body listening and available, even when it's stressing me out.

And yes, showing up fully will mean making mistakes. Likely causing some wounds. Perhaps being wounded ourselves.

But at least the ones we love will know we are there.

CONCLUSION

I am a confusing mixture of boiling anxiety and delusional hope. This is experienced most clearly when deciding to rid my house of a spider but forgetting to do it. One part of me happy that the spider has escaped my vacuum cleaner and will live his life freely and the other part fearful that it will crawl into my mouth while I sleep.

I felt the same way as I wrote this compilation. One part in full belief that it would be a fulfillment of my life's calling. Another part already writing out the bad reviews before I ever typed a word: "Her prose was witty, but she is stupid," or "I follow her online but had no idea that she'd ever said a curse word, and I'm shocked and appalled to read about it here."

However, the delusional hope kept this process alive, and for that, I am eternally grateful.

I believe that conversations like the one we are having here are integral to the healing of ourselves and our society. I hope these essays and poems can serve as a balm and, at times, a challenge as we seek to find more love, patience, and peace in our own lives. I hope that they serve as a reminder that you are not alone in your journey of being human as well as an invitation to swipe away the categorizations and limitations of who you thought you had to be.

Because, at the end of the day, you are not your Enneagram type. You are a living, breathing, complicated individual who has a myriad of experiences, pains, and joys that have formed you into the being you are. You are, in essence, a complicated and beautiful individual who cannot be summed up in a simple typing system. In fact, the Enneagram is your ticket out of the compartment that you've limited yourself to.

YOU—the real you—are so much more than a number.

ACKNOWLEDGMENTS

I want to say thank you first to my husband, Oby Arnold, for letting me read every single word of this book aloud to him as I wrote, for believing in me more than I believe in myself, and for being the one who wipes the tears and sweat from my brow as I do the things I'm scared of doing. I am better for having been loved by you.

Thank you to my dear friends, Tyler McCall, Eric Campbell, and Laura Lee, for sitting with me as I talked through ideas, titles, and business plans.

Thank you to my editor, Katie Gould, for your support, feedback, and encouragement. Thanks for working with me on another one!

Andrews McMeel Publishing
a division of Andrews McMeel Universal
1130 Walnut Street, Kansas City, Missouri 64106

www.andrewsmcmeel.com

22 23 24 25 26 SDB 10 9 8 7 6 5 4 3 2 1

ISBN: 978-1-5248-7569-5

Library of Congress Control Number: 2022937043

Editor: Katie Gould
Art Director: Holly Swayne
Production Editor: Meg Utz
Production Manager: Tamara Haus

ATTENTION: SCHOOLS AND BUSINESSES
Andrews McMeel books are available at quantity discounts with bulk
purchase for educational, business, or sales promotional use. For information,
please e-mail the Andrews McMeel Publishing Special Sales Department:
specialsales@amuniversal.com.